THE PULPIT
REDISCOVERS THEOLOGY

✠ ✠ ✠

THEODORE O. WEDEL

✠ ✠ ✠

The Pulpit
Rediscovers Theology

GREENWICH · CONNECTICUT

1956

Printed in the United States of America
Designed by Nancy H. Dale

Dedicated
to the memory of
The Right Reverend George Craig Stewart,
Bishop of Chicago, 1930-1940,
who gave to the pulpit its rightful authority
in the common life of the people of God

The themes of several chapters of this book received their first presentation under the George Craig Stewart Memorial Lectureship, at the Seabury-Western Seminary, Evanston, Illinois.

PREFACE

✠ ✠ ✠

There can be no doubt that ours is an age of glorious theological recovery. The Queen of the sciences is once more on her long forsaken throne. And the proof of our being in the midst of a flowering of theological rediscovery of the wonders of our heritage of Christian faith is nowhere more clearly seen than in the return of interest and understanding of the Bible—a Bible which has miraculously survived centuries of often painful and disillusioning historical scrutiny. Indeed, no formula is more commonly used today to define our theological climate than the phrase "biblical theology."

The problem confronting the preacher today is that of appropriating for the nurture of his flock this wealth of fresh theological insight. A recent observer, also expressing gratitude for the theological revival of our time, especially as this has given us back our Bible, sadly remarks: "The rediscovery of the Bible as the source book of theology has not gone far enough—it has not reached the pulpit. Brilliant exceptions may here and there be witnessed, but they serve to point up the lack of biblical basis in the average contemporary sermon." [1]

My brethren of the clergy—among whom this volume hopes to find at least some readers—will note that it is critical of much contemporary preaching. It has been my vocation for a decade and more to preside over an institution (The College of Preachers of Washington Cathedral) devoted to the ministry of the pulpit. Clergy (of the Episcopal Church) are invited to the College in groups of twenty-five for a week of theological refreshment, but also for undergoing the discipline of preaching before their fellow ministers and of having their sermons subjected to criticism.

I realize that, as a professional "sermon listener," I have long since endangered my soul's salvation by yielding to the mood of censoriousness. And I must confess that in this book I present the problems faced by the contemporary preacher with the diagnosis of the dangers more prominently portrayed than the signs of the return of "the lost authority of the pulpit," although these signs, I am more than willing to prophesy, are even now on the horizon. It is simply honesty to confess that we, the custodians in the Church of the ministry of the Word, have been the legatees of a century and more of theological confusion. Dependent as we are upon the masters in the schools to give us our anchorage in the Christian faith in our youth, we find ourselves, in this era of theological advance into new

[1] "Biblical Theology and the Pulpit," an editorial in *Interpretation* (Richmond, Virginia), October, 1951.

lands of promise, often lagging a generation behind the
march of the theological pioneers.

The chapters of this book are revised versions of materials that I have been privileged to present in lectures before theological seminary assemblies and clergy
groups. I venture to name specifically the Seabury-
Western Seminary in Evanston, Illinois, the Andover
Newton Seminary in Massachusetts, the Princeton
Theological Seminary in New Jersey, and the Moravian
Seminary in Bethlehem, Pennsylvania, and to express
here gratitude for patient listening. The closing chapter
is a reprint (by permission) of the Ingersoll Lecture
delivered at the Harvard Divinity School in the spring
of 1954, which is receiving separate publication in the
Harvard Divinity School Bulletin. An article, entitled,
"The Lost Authority of the Pulpit," which appeared in
Theology Today (June, 1952), also contained some
treatment of a theme now repeated in this volume.

This volume is designed to help the preacher who is
conscious of failure in utilizing fully the promise of a
"Bible rediscovered" to come into his rightful inheritance. For those who are already at home in the rediscovered world of "biblical theology," this book will be
a threshing of old straw. Indeed, however humbling to
the author, its design will have been fulfilled when it
will itself be clearly out of date.

THEODORE O. WEDEL

CONTENTS

✠ ✠ ✠

CHAPTER I

Our Bewildered Pulpit

The minister sits at his study desk. Next Sunday's sermon looms. He wrestles with the "how" and the "what" of preaching.

The "how" of preaching is a perennial problem, of course. The making of sermons is an art that is never perfected. Few of us are great preachers. But our problem is not chiefly technical, for a knowledge of the principles of sermon construction is not impossible to acquire. Every preacher, after a few years in the pulpit, could write his own textbook on sermon making. He has wrestled scores of times with the homiletic ritual of introduction, body, and conclusion. It is not ignorance of the form a good sermon takes that burdens his conscience as he sits at his desk. If memorizing the rules of sonnet construction could produce great poetry, the world would not have had to wait for the genius of a Shakespeare or a Milton. No, the preacher's agony of creation has far deeper roots. He must choose a text or theme. He must have something to say—a "message," as our elders in the ministry were wont to call it.[1] He must draw water of life for his congregation from the well of his imagination and conviction and personal faith, as well as from the Bible, the faith of the Church, and the treasure house of Christian theology.

The Minister's Awesome Concern

Sermons grow only in a minister's meditative life—during the quiet hours spent in the presence of God, when the Holy Spirit has opportunity to lead those who listen into all truth. Without the help of what George Fox used to call "openings"—a breaking in of insights into a truth of faith—sermons become mere homiletic hackwork. But "openings" demand reflective hours, which are not easily won in the whirl of a minister's busy administrative and pastoral toil. Accordingly, the minister at his desk groans under his burden of guilt. Where is he, a sinner, to find for his waiting flock words that shall be worthily called words of the Lord?

The preacher may well marvel that his congregation somehow gathers week by week, on the Lord's Day, to listen to his fumbling homily. He would gladly welcome a moratorium on preaching, his own at least. True, he may receive comfort from the fact that a congregation's worship of God is not confined to sermon listening—

[1] One of Karl Barth's earliest writings to be translated into English—*The Word of God and the Word of Man* (Boston: The Pilgrim Press, 1928), pp. 79ff.—vividly describes this awesome concern of the preacher when he stands in his pulpit.

as, indeed, it is not—yet he knows that a neglect of
the pulpit leads to a neglect of prayer and sacrament as
well. "How then shall they call on him in whom they
have not believed? and how shall they believe in him
of whom they have not heard?" (Rom. 10:14) When
there is no understanding of their meaning in the
drama of redemption, sacraments can turn into mere
magical rites. And prayer, if left to itself and if not
addressed to the true God of the Christian revelation,
can become a demonic force for evil.[2] There is no escape, even for the pastoral and priestly ministry, from
the ministry of the Word.

Concern over the "how" of preaching, accordingly,
yields first place to the "what" of the preacher's message.
As he wrestles with the content of his sermon, the
minister's agony becomes truly acute. He faces today
a bewildered world, a bewildered congregation. I spare
the reader a description of its tragedy and pain, its loss
of faith and hope. We, of the remnants of Christendom,
may come to resemble the citizens of fifth century Rome,
with barbarian hordes trampling down a millennium of

[2] "Prayer as such is not necessarily a good thing. Unless it is
directed to the right Person in the way He has laid down, it
can become a demonic force and do untold damage to man and
nation. . . . The whole history of the race testifies to the ambiguity of prayer. It can be a highly dangerous thing, the most
subtle and effective means of hiding man from the face of
God. . . . For a natural human prayer is always an attempt to have
God on man's terms." Quoted from an invaluable book on prayer:
Daniel T. Jenkins, *Prayer and the Service of God* (New York:
Morehouse-Gorham Co., 1945), pp. 17 and 34. Used by permission of the publisher.

culture; or those of the later Europe who witnessed a victorious Islam at the gates of Vienna. The possibility is not fanciful. A preacher today needs merely to present the modern world's disillusionments by title, and these will be readily recognized, even when his listeners refuse to face them and cry for opiates or gospels of escape. Allusions to atom or hydrogen bombs still, no doubt, furnish purple passages for our sermons, but such allusions have long since ceased to be news. Sad news, in truth, needs little underscoring in the pulpit today. The fear of the future or of blind Fate, if not fear of the Lord, is abroad in the land. It is at least *fear,* and may turn into what the Bible calls right fear—godly fear, which is "the beginning of wisdom." It is background in our time for the pitiful, all-pervading hunger for good news, for a gospel.

Good News! Does the preacher in his study possess it? Or does a bewildered pulpit confront a bewildered world?

The Preacher's Bookshelf

The preacher at his desk, we may presume, casts his eye over the books on his shelves. There they are: volumes on systematic theology, church history, liturgics, Christian biography, prayer and the devotional life, the social gospel or its modern equivalents—all this in addition to the Bible itself, commentary helps, and a probably heterogeneous collection of secular literatures. But can these books give him the help he needs?

The preacher will, no doubt, choose sermon themes on occasions from among the hundred and one topical interests of the hour. When illuminated by insight into God's own Word to man, what, indeed, can be more helpful than such contemporaneous preaching? We need today, someone has suggested, Christian laymen who can read their newspapers theologically. Yet most of us soon overreach ourselves when we try to rival the political or social commentators of the day even when it is at Christian commentary we aim. We are not experts in international diplomacy or in banking or even in the intricate legal and legislative problems relating to social service or community welfare. We may, indeed, take our stand on issues of the hour—alcoholism, a labor-management dispute, pacifism, or any one of the hundreds of interesting current topics before the public. But our parishioners rightly rebel when we, mere fallible mortals like themselves, presume to play the role of God in their lives. They must make their own decisions. They look to us not for inexpert advice as to how to vote in an election, but for light from another world on this world—light in which they can receive the courage to decide for right against wrong as they, in the depths of conscience, already see it. They feel a need, fully acknowledged or not, for being brought into judgment, for the healing that alone can come from facing their own guilt-burdened lives, and for the divine truth which can set them free. Why else should they bother to come into the presence of the holy God in His house on the Lord's Day at all? The preacher need not shirk the text of Amos: "For three transgressions . . . Yea, for four, I will not turn away the punishment thereof" (Amos 2:6, ASV), applying it to the social scene and the social sins of our time. We men of God have the right and duty to arouse conscience to the point of repentance and, possibly, even of despair. But we must leave conscience free.

In addition to topical sermons, the preacher will rightly be led to choose themes from out of what can be called the peripheral realms of Gospel truth—Christian biography, Church history, and, above all, the Christian cult. The latter especially yields rich fruitage of Christian understanding. Great value attaches to sermons on the "sacraments of the Gospel," baptism and the Lord's Supper, for example. Surely, we need not leave homiletic instruction on the Christian cult to Roman Catholics! One of the explanations of why Rome retains a hold on her children is, clearly, Rome's cult discipline and the foundations of careful pedagogic training upon which cult loyalty is built. I shall not here enlarge upon the value of such sermon themes.[3] This value is obvious when seen in the light of a fully rounded understanding of Christian faith and life. But cult loyalty and understanding, as a wise Romanist would be the first to assert, can flourish rightly only in

[3] The value of sermons on the Christian sacraments is discussed in Chapter V.

the soil of previously implanted dogmatic convictions. Eventually, obedience to Church discipline and full participation in her sacramental life depend upon the preaching of the Gospel itself.

We are back, then, in the preacher's study as he seeks for his message. He, too, knows that sooner or later, when topical or peripheral themes have had their day, or have been exhausted, he must turn for the enduring substance of his preaching to the rock upon which the Church, of which he is priest and prophet, is herself founded—the Church's *Faith*, the Church's Gospel.

Two resources for light on the faith of the Church lie ready to the preacher's hand. The first is, obviously, the Bible itself. The second is Christian dogma, embodied in creed, confessions, and textbooks on systematic theology. To which will he turn, or can he use them both?

The Secularist Revolution

In days when the Church, both Catholic and Protestant, was as yet untroubled by the scientific era and its doubt of the miraculous in the biblical record, a conflict between dogma and Bible was unknown. Bible and dogma were, in a real sense, one and the same. An "undogmatic" Gospel was almost inconceivable. Jesus, to cite the clue example, was the Christ of St. Paul, as well as the Nazarene rabbi of the Evangelists. Neither theologians nor pulpit preachers worried about the prob-

lem "Jesus *or* Paul." The life of Christ, when taught
and preached, was the New Testament life of Christ
as a whole. He was chief actor in a great redemption
story—an action involving heaven and earth and even
hell—one in which Deity for the love of fallen man
"came down from heaven," died, rose from a grave,
ascended to heaven, and, by His return as Holy Spirit,
prepared His people for the final act in the drama, a
second coming "to judge the quick and the dead."
The cosmological framework within which theologian,
preacher, and listening congregation envisioned the
events of all the biblical narratives was a three-story
universe. Secularism, or the view of man's existence
limited to a one-story universe, was an ethical alterna-
tive for a medieval or classical Protestant Christian, of
course, as for man in any age, but it was not an alterna-
tive for him as a philosophical or theological reality.
Even pagan man would not have understood it, for he,
too, still believed in gods upon their thrones and saw
man's life *sub specie aeternitatis.*

Today, all this is changed. Secularism is the normal
framework for modern man's thought and action. It has
invaded theology itself, and especially the interpretation
of the Bible. In some forms, to be sure, it does not deny
the existence of a God, or even a possible relationship
with Him, or God's continued action in history, since
it still retains a remnant—a spiritualized and shadow
remnant, one could say—of the older three-story universe. Heaven has become the realm of human ideals,

the goal of human aspiration. Hell has been transmuted
into immortality. The old wine of biblical imagery is
thus poured into new bottles; and both Bible and traditional Christian dogma is, indeed, honored on formal
occasions as of old, and their hallowed vocabulary and
imagery utilized in preaching. But the change that has
taken place, when properly understood, is, nevertheless,
momentous. For the Bible has, in reality, been reduced
to the story of religious man and his climb upward
toward Deity; it has ceased to be the story of God Himself, speaking in the Law and through the Prophets,
and Himself invading man's world as "Word made
flesh."

Dogmatic Theology

What this revolution means for both pulpit and pew
must be left for later discussion. Suffice it to say, at
the moment, that the modern preacher faces a dilemma
unknown to his grandfathers in the ministry. He must
make a choice, so it would appear, between Bible and
Christian Creed, between exegesis of a Bible text as
seen through the eyes of traditional Christian dogma
and that same text emancipated from such dogmatic
tyranny. Older generations of Christian evangelists, as
already hinted, would have thought such a dilemma
impossible. Many contemporary preachers also think
that it is impossible or that it can be safely ignored;
they are not aware of the fact that a choice is confront-

ing them. They are making a fateful decision, nevertheless.

Dogmatic or systematic theology has, to be sure,
never been wholly domesticated in the pulpit. The Bible
first, with systematic theology a distant second—this
has surely been a healthy pedagogic principle for Christian preachers from the days of Chrysostom to that of
Moody. We do not choose *texts* from the writings of
Augustine or Thomas Aquinas or Luther or Calvin or
Hooker or Karl Barth or Reinhold Niebuhr. Furthermore, it is, in a sense, precisely the preacher's duty to
protect his flock from the heresy that Christianity consists of intellectual systems of belief. Kierkegaard rightly
poured scorn on mere "professor-Christianity." St. Paul
castigated it in his Epistle to the Colossians, and praised
the "foolishness of preaching" (I Cor. 1:21). Jesus
Himself once set a child in the midst of the disciples, as
a model for entrance into the kingdom of heaven (Matt.
8:3), and, on another occasion, He thanked His heavenly Father that "thou didst hide these things from the
wise and understanding, and didst reveal them unto
babes" (Matt. 11:25, ASV). Clearly, the suspicion of
the wilderness of theological warfare that simple Bible
Christians have is partly justified. Some of us may recall the delightful cartoon in *Punch*, picturing a learned
divine leaning over his pulpit and addressing a group
of villagers with the words: "Now *you* will say, this
is Sabellianism!" Where is the preacher who would
affront his parishioners with a learned discourse on

"Supralapsarianism"; yet only recently Karl Barth, in his monumental textbook on dogmatic theology, devotes many careful pages to this theologically important topic.[4]

Other indictments, from the point of view of the preacher, against the learned doctors of the Church and their, at times, unbearable professional remoteness and even haughty intellectual snobbery lie ready to hand. *"They* are safe in their ivory towers of abstractions," so the indictment goes. *"We* deal with living men and women for whom doing is more important than thinking, as it ought surely to be for all Christians. Faith is obedience and discipleship, not wearisome wrestling with the doctrine of the two natures of Christ or the clashing theories of the Atonement. To place the Bible and Christian faith under the overlordship of a theological system, furthermore, is to surrender their power. Dogmas are impersonal. Christian allegiance belongs to the Person of Christ, not doctrines about Him. Anything less is what the theologians themselves call 'heteronomy' (an alien law)." Or again: "The systems of theology in our textbooks are tradition-bound. We cry for an apologetic for today. The learned doctors, from New Testament days to our own, seem to have written books that can be read and understood only by other theologians, not by the layman or the simple preacher. Frequently, they seem to disguise their igno-

---

[4] Karl Barth, *Kirchliche Dogmatik* (Zurich: Evangelischer Verlag Zollikon, 1942), Vol. II, pages 136ff.

rance by long quotations, equally ignorant, out of a long-dead past. Contrast these elaborate dogmatic systems with the Bible itself. Can you find any theological systems anywhere in the Old Testament, or in the teachings of Jesus, or even, in any such technical forms as appear in our textbooks, in the writings of St. Paul or the early Church? [5] If the apostolic age or humble believers through the centuries could live without such systems, why cannot we?"

Our Theological Revival

Thus runs the indictment, and thus may run many a preacher's self-defense, as he contemplates by-passing his library shelf with its volumes on systematic divinity. I doubt, however, that he will succeed in his, possibly

[5] An elaboration of the above brief indictment of "Dogmatics" can be found in Emil Brunner's masterly *Dogmatik* (Zurich: Zwingli-Verlag), I, 6-16. Brunner proceeds, of course, to define and defend systematic theology against these partially legitimate charges. Dogmatic theology is, so he rightly argues, an essential function of the Church's existence in history:

1. Without it, Christian faith would long ago have succumbed to heresy.
2. Baptismal instruction *must* assume some kind of systematic expression.
3. No exegesis of the Bible itself is possible without the unfolding of dogmatic implications.
4. In the final analysis, the Bible does *not* obviously explain itself. It requires interpretation, and this is dogmatic theology. The real issue, then, becomes the battle between right dogmatics and wrong dogmatics, right theology and wrong theology. This issue is the substance of the remainder of Brunner's volume—as it is of all serious theological debate.

habitual, neglect of theology with an altogether clear conscience. If he is keeping abreast, even casually, with contemporary religious literature, he knows that theology—dogmatic theology, at that—is no longer a Cinderella in a back kitchen, as it seemed to be a generation ago, but has been transformed into the belle of the ball. The Queen of the sciences, to vary the figure, has suddenly resumed her seat on her throne. The restoration, so it appears, began in the Protestant theology of continental Europe, Karl Barth being a conspicuous, though not isolated, pioneer; it has since spread over the non-Romanist world, with Rome herself not unmoved. Translations of books in German on systematic theology are pouring from the presses of England and America today, as did the translations of scholars in the field of historical study of the Bible a generation ago. Nor is this revolution limited to the continental schools of theology. Scotland, England, and America have joined the parade back to dogmatic theological wrestling. The writings of Peter Taylor Forsyth—sometimes called "an English Barth before Barth"—are being reissued and resurrected from ill-deserved neglect. He has brilliant followers, in the line of English Free Church theology, in J. S. Whale, C. H. Dodd, Vincent Taylor, D. T. Jenkins, and many more. In Scotland there are John Baillie and Donald Baillie. Anglicanism, though still much occupied with ecclesiological and cultic interests, contributes the writings of Leonard Hodgson, Edwyn Hoskyns, William Temple,

L. S. Thornton, and A. G. Hebert. And on the American scene, who has not read at least samplings of the writings of Paul Tillich or the brothers Niebuhr (Reinhold and Richard) or Edwin Lewis or John Mackay, and of their colleagues and followers?

The reader of current theological literature can note another fact that may be for him either hopeful or disturbing. The "new" theology—if a revival of classical Christian thought deserves to be labelled a novelty—has itself returned to the Bible. A generation ago, biblical study was still largely in the hands of historians rather than theologians. Many of the lives of Jesus, for example, and books dealing with the New Testament record of His teachings and place in history had, as their specific aim, the rescue of Christianity's Founder from the rubble-heap of warring dogmatic systems under which He seemingly had lain buried throughout most of Christian history.[6] Even the epistles of the New Testament—above all, those of St. Paul—were demoted from their once unquestioned position of theological authority. St. Paul and his theology was not read out of the New Testament, of course, but Pauline dogmatic thought was explained historically as simply another proof—this time subsequent to the life of Jesus as such—of His overpowering personality and the abid-

[6] As late as 1901, a competent observer could say, "It is a most significant fact that every single life of Christ since the Gospels is the product of the last sixty-five years." Henry Churchill King, *Reconstruction in Theology* (New York: The Macmillan Co., 1901), p. 186.

ing influence that Jesus exercised upon His followers. The dogma emerging in the New Testament epistles, according to this theory, could be honored as evidence of the centrality of Jesus for all future history, but this dogma should not becloud the story of Jesus Himself. An "undogmatic Christ" could be recaptured by historic search and given lordship over dogma. A "historic Jesus" replaced the "Christ of theology" as the object of Christian devotion.

The Queen of the Sciences Returns

Many of us who stand in pulpits today have been reared in the classrooms of beloved teachers who brought us into the presence of the Jesus of the incomparable Gospel record and made His human person the center of our loyalty and of our preaching. Even those of us who have more recently passed through an academic course and have felt the impact of the theological revolution now upsetting the calm of seminary lecture halls and common rooms, have felt the romantic spell of the "historic Jesus" cult. Pulpit traditions of at least half a century have paid homiletic tribute to this version of the Christian faith.

That is the reason the new winds blowing through the theological academe leave us bewildered. Did something go wrong in the era when Christian revelation became a monopoly of historians? Whatever the answer may be, dogmatic theologians are today challenging that reign of historicism. And this revived dogmatic theology is a chastened theology. Although one can prophesy that never again will dogmatic theology be able to ignore the critical results of the historian's searching eye, one must also grant that dogmatic theology is today confronting the now traditional "historical Jesus" Christianity with a peremptory "no." "Back to St. Paul. Back to a dogmatic Christ," are the slogans.

And it is precisely in the name of the Bible itself that this revolution is finding its power—the Bible regarded and accepted once more as theological revelation, not as mere history without dogma. The "new" theology goes by many names—neo-orthodoxy, Barthianism, the new evangelicalism, and several more—and is a diverse movement that cannot be thought of as the monopoly of a single theologian or of a school. Quite possibly, the best term to express the nature of the movement is *biblical theology,* with emphasis falling on both terms. We are back to the Bible, but we are at the same time back to theology, in the traditional, dogmatic sense of the word.

A notable book on the New Testament concludes with this lyric note:

These are great days for theology. The Queen of the sciences is once again coming into her own. Men are beginning to see that a Christianity without a theology is not Christianity at all; and they are turning back, some to Luther or Calvin, some to Thomas Aquinas. Some of us, with no disrespect for these great names, feel that the theology which the age needs should be built primarily on New Testament foundations. But, whatever be our views, all are realizing anew the importance of Biblical theology.[7]

The New Testament, it should be noted, however, is now no longer divided between a biography of Jesus and a theological commentary that can be accorded a secondary role. The New Testament is once more considered as a whole, its theology being an integral part of its drama and story and, thus, of its authority as revelation. The conviction is now boldly voiced that it is a unity and not disjunctive parts, that "through it runs one message, that from its beginning to its end there is a grand agreement concerning the 'so great salvation' of which every one of its writers speaks." [8]

I have sketched here, in roughest outline only, the theological revolution of our time. We shall have to return to a consideration of it repeatedly in the following chapters. But let us, at this point, return to our preacher at his desk. If he is a reading man at all, and one of sensitive conscience, he realizes that he cannot permanently ignore the major prophets of our generation. Sooner or later their message will penetrate the walls of his study and challenge his sermons and the gospel he is preaching. Yet bewilderment often continues to be his prevailing mood, for while he knows he

[7] Archibald M. Hunter, *The Message of the New Testament* (Philadelphia: The Westminster Press, 1944), p. 122. Used by permission of the publisher.
[8] *Ibid.*

cannot go back to the fundamentalist biblical literalism of earlier centuries, he finds this new orthodoxy, however biblical it may claim to be, often strange and baffling. He has tried, perhaps, a sermon or two on "sin à la Niebuhr," or, if he has been caught up in the now fashionable Kierkegaard cult, he has tried several sermons on "anxiety." The new psychology has also offered alluring themes for his sermons—themes susceptible to theological treatment. He may even have resurrected and reread his seminary notebooks on systematic theology and been happy to find that he can, on the whole, still subscribe in loyalty to the Church's standards of faith and that he need not count himself a heretic.

Can We Preach Dogma?

But to preach all this—that is a different matter. He has tried it on festival days like Trinity Sunday when he gave his congregation a heavy dose of straight doctrine. In sermons on Christmas, Good Friday, Easter and Pentecost (Ascension Day, fortunately, rarely demanding a sermon), some wrestling with the dogmatic meaning of these events in the framework of the Christian story was unavoidable, but it was always hard going. Many a preacher would probably admit that his poorest sermons or, at least, those most difficult for him to construct were those to be given on the major festivals of the Church Year. Traditional Christian dogma simply took the miraculous in the Bible naively in its stride.

But we cannot possibly do this today. The contemporary masters of theology who beckon us to return to a dogmatic Bible seem to solve the major problems of the supernatural and miraculous in the Bible by terming them "mythology" or by leaving the historical questions altogether alone, and by basing their conclusion simply on what they term "apostolic faith," "the Church's faith," or "the faith of the New Testament." But try preaching "mythology" from the pulpit to an unsophisticated congregation!

We of an older generation were taught to start with unquestioned historic fact and to proceed from there to construct whatever minimum doctrinal framework appeared necessary to furnish intelligible background. These newer theologians seem to reverse the process. They accept Christianity as a faith first, and then take for granted that sufficient trustworthy historic facts preceded the faith to anchor it in history. Their treatment of the Resurrection furnishes a good example. The whole Bible, and not only the excerpts vouched for by the literalist historian, can thus again come to life. But it would take a revolution in our preaching to prepare our lay folk for such an understanding of Christianity. We are, most of us, simply not equipped for it. A gulf has perhaps always existed in Christian history between the learned doctors of the schools and the simple preachers of the Gospel. Today the gulf is wide. Middlemen are needed to translate theological insight into usable homiletic material.

In fact, the age-old distrust of the abstractions of scholastic theology has not disappeared. Even when the preacher has made himself familiar with current theological thought, he often feels that he must stand to one side. The professors are not agreed. Dr. Brunner and Dr. Barth, to cite one example, cry "no" to each other.[9] Who are we to take sides or to burden our congregations with the warfare of theology?

We are, accordingly, if we honestly confess to our state, a bewildered lot. If we cannot return to a literalist Bible and if the rediscovered Christianity of dogma is as yet for us alien and strange, have we anything left? Next Sunday's sermon, clearly, cannot wait until we have taken time out for a postgraduate course in dogmatics.

Undogmatic Preaching

Most of us, I suspect, will yield to habit and to the pulpit tradition of the last half century, and will turn to our Bibles for an undogmatic text. The historian and moralist in us will have conquered the theologian. Surely, so we comfort ourselves, this is the world with which our people are familiar—the world of moral strife. "Conduct," Matthew Arnold has reminded us, "is three-fourths of life." Our parishioners are not theolo-

[9] A readable account of this theological debate can be found in John Baillie's *Our Knowledge of God* (New York: C. Scribner's Sons, 1939).

gians either. They need practical guidance—to be told
things they can do—and the uplift of Christian ideals.
We shall even preach Christ to them, but it will be a
Christ they can understand. We shall picture Him as
Master and Friend and Brother, and as Example. Some
day they and we may come to know Him well enough
to appreciate the dogma about Him. But that can wait.

Two large realms of biblical truth and biblical texts,
accordingly, are left us: 1. the ethical imperatives of the
New Testament, above all the teachings of Jesus; and
2. the life of Christ of the Evangelists and the resultant
portrayal of His personality. Nor are we limited, in our
choice of biblical material, to Matthew, Mark, and Luke.
Ethical moralism runs all through the Bible. We can
preach the personalities of the Old Testament. We can
preach large sections of the epistles without getting
bogged down by doctrinal puzzles. Even St. Paul, when
he gets through with his theological wrestlings on law
and grace and justification and his "Christ-mysticism,"
always comes out with plain, practical ethics at the
end—Romans 12-15 being a perfect example. This is
the point at which we and our people can enter.

Hence Christian ethical idealism and practical moralizing are likely to form the substance of most of our
sermons. We can take the parables, for example. The
New Testament itself appears to give us a model as to
how they may be moralized in the Parable of the Sower,
which becomes the parable of the "soils." The mere
recital of it yields a challenge to the indifferent in our

congregations. Clearly they are being asked to become other than stony or thorny ground for the reception of the seed of the Gospel. Other parables yield similar homiletic material, obviously moralistic. The Parable of the Good Samaritan ties in with the command to love one's neighbor.[10] Mustard seed and leaven can be utilized to show the amazing results of good deeds in a naughty world. Not all parables, to be sure, are exegetically quite so easy to handle. At times we may even suspect that theology lurks in these matchless stories.[11] The Parable of the Prodigal Son plainly goes beyond ethics and taps deeper levels of experience. But this is, apparently, an exception. Even the Parable of the Pharisee and the Publican—which, with its attack on salvation by works, reads almost like something St. Paul might have written—can be retained within the framework of moralistic interpretation. It becomes a story-sermon against pride.

And the parables are, of course, only a fraction of the ethical documents of the New Testament. There is, above all, the Sermon on the Mount and allied sayings of Jesus. The suspicion is not unwarranted that we refer to this Sermon on the Mount more frequently as a whole and by way of generalized allusion than in detail.

[10] For a non-moralistic and "theological" interpretation of this parable, see page 97ff.

[11] As, indeed, it does! Biblical theologians are beginning to show us that all the parables are theology, and not moral tales. The best commentary on the parables of Jesus is, quite possibly, the Epistle to the Romans. Jesus and Paul taught the same theology!

Exegesis of its separate sections presents difficulties. We use it most easily when we paint a contrast between the positive idealism of the New Testament as against the mere negative "thou shalt not" of Moses and the jealous God of the Old Testament. It opens the door to the picturing of the ideals of the Christian life. The New Testament is filled with such perfectionist portraits. Here St. Paul's description of what he calls life "in Christ" supplements the Sermon on the Mount and the Beatitudes and Jesus' own picture of the kingdom of heaven. If we present this ideal vividly enough in our sermons, so we may have convinced ourselves, it cannot fail to win converts. All of the homiletic talents we possess must be harnessed to this task of persuasion.

The Imitation of Jesus

Our chief resource in preaching our perfectionist ethic is, finally, the life of Christ Himself. By His *life* we mean, of course, the story told by the Evangelists. Many details of this biography remain mysterious and must be left unexamined; yet enough of the simple humanity and moral grandeur of Jesus is left to assure His making an overwhelming moral appeal. This appeal will result, in its effect upon our hearers, we trust, in imitation and discipleship.

Few words in the vocabulary of modern preaching carry so much of the authority of homiletic tradition as the word "discipleship." It summarizes by itself, so it clearly seems, the whole of Christianity's message. Let the professors in the schools fight their doctrinal battles. Let their *odium theologicum* rage. They, too, if they ever emerge from their verbal wind-tunnels, must come to discipleship as a final resultant. Why then should we not circumvent the dogmatic Christological debates and accept what dogma, too, must finally yield —the challenge of the imitation of Jesus.

The connotations of the word discipleship, accordingly, can furnish substance for hundreds of sermons. The life of Christ—thought of again as limited to the years between His birth and death—can be presented in detail. The miracle stories, even when we leave them as historical puzzles, can portray Christ's humanitarian zeal. His obedience to His heavenly Father, even to martyrdom on the Cross, can be for us a supernal example, as it was unquestionably for the early Church (I Pet. 2:21). Cross-bearing is a theme touching the lives of every man, woman, and child in our congregations. We can set before them One who showed us how to turn our crosses into victories as His spirit emerged victorious from His Cross by inspiring His followers to become a serving and cross-bearing fellowship. Nor need discipleship limit itself to ethical heroism. It can enter into imitation of Jesus as religious genius as well —His sublime trust in His and our heavenly Father, His prayer life, and His forgiveness of His fellow men, a forgiveness which He assured us was like that of God. It is no wonder that His followers, particularly after His death, made of Him a kind of second God and called Him Lord and began to weave into the pattern of His biography theological terminology. His spirit was not holden of the grave. It can live today in our hearts and lead us through contemplation of His person to God. The dogmas *about* Jesus—that of His divinity above all—can be accepted by us as proofs of what He once meant to His disciples. We, however, need not burden our sermons or our parishioners with these dogmatic speculations. If they help in leading men to discipleship, well and good. But, clearly, it is discipleship which finally counts and which defines our relationship to the Founder of our Christian faith. All else simply must be secondary. We can thank our modern scholars for unveiling the historical Jesus for us so vividly that He can again make His own appeal across the centuries, without the grave-clothes of dogma.

The above sketch of the anchorage of much modern preaching may, at times, border upon caricature, for most of us can produce from our files sermons which deal with biblical concepts on a deeper level than moralism or even discipleship. Yet I suspect that such an analysis (it could be greatly expanded) is not wholly mistaken. I, at least, can testify that I have listened to hundreds of sermons which, whatever be their point of departure, reach this as a climax—Christ-imitation as an imperative. The closing paragraphs of our sermons are frequently *we must* paragraphs.

Are doubts as to the adequacy of this version of the

Christian Gospel beginning to arrive? I suspect that they are. The theologians are disturbing our calm as we sit at our study desks. And even when we leave their works unread on our library shelves, our experience in the pastoral ministry is enough to arouse in us questionings about our preaching. Is this *we must* gospel of ours meeting the real needs of our people? I venture to list a few at least of the doubts as to our message which, sooner or later, we may be called upon to face.

Doubts and Questionings

First of all, we cannot fail to be aware of the fact that we are anthologizing our Bibles. We have enthroned the Synoptic Gospels to almost exclusive lordship over the rest of Scripture. This seems at first to be obviously right. Christianity is centered on Jesus or it is not Christianity at all. But if it should turn out that the historic Jesus whom we think we meet in Matthew, Mark, and Luke, should be the same Jesus whom the early Church preached as the divine Son of God, we are at once in difficulties. That apostolic age wrote the Gospel narratives. Did they preach two different Christs—the historic Jesus on the one hand and the Christ of faith on the other? Turn to the New Testament from the Book of the Acts through the Apocalypse and there is no trace of such a dichotomy. Indeed, the preaching of the apostolic era seems to have concentrated upon the second of the two "Christs." Have we of the twentieth century the right to reverse all this? Are we, possibly, trying to create a *new* Christian religion?

A second doubt can come to the modern preacher when and if he reminds himself of the root meaning of the word "gospel." He uses the word, no doubt, freely enough. Is he true to its joyous connotation "good news"? The *we musts* of our sermons, are they good news? Is the perfectionist ethic of our version of Jesus' teaching exactly good news? Is discipleship, if demanded seriously of our people and not merely presented as a sentimental appeal, good news? Is the Sermon on the Mount, if again taken seriously as a moral code which we are not only expected to admire but to perform, good news? A recent theological student of the New Testament has called it "the most terrible indictment of human nature ever written. There is no account of sin to match that of the Sermon.' " [12]

A third doubt, related to the previous one, can attach itself to the word "discipleship" itself. The imitation of Christ and the concept of discipleship are unquestionably deeply anchored in the whole of the New Testament portrayal of the Christian life. But, if we indulge in a little careful exegesis and use our concordances, there is something strange about discipleship, also. The word itself does not occur in the epistles of the New Testament! A surprising fact, surely, and one which, if it be followed far enough, can unlock for us some of

[12] Archibald M. Hunter, *The Message of the New Testament* (Philadelphia: The Westminster Press, 1944), p. 92.

the secrets of authentic New Testament Christianity. We may not be called upon to drop the use of the word, but we are called upon to give it a deepened meaning.

One clue to the puzzle surrounding discipleship can be seen plainly in the Gospels themselves. It was not discipleship, in the moralistic sense of the word, at least, that turned the followers of Jesus into Christians. Something else had to happen beyond intimate contact with the rabbi of Nazareth to transform the disciple-group into apostles, witnesses, and martyrs. How much value would Peter, on the night of his betrayal of Jesus, have placed on his achievements in discipleship? The power to imitate Christ came to him later as apostle from sources far beyond those he had known in the days when he companioned (as you and I will never be able to companion) with Jesus as Master. And it is clearly this "plus" in the story, these acts in the drama which came after the death of Jesus, that were central in apostolic faith—Resurrection, Ascension, and Pentecost; it is these that account for the resultant revolution in the life of the disciple-group. Yet this nexus of events and the faith dependent upon these events constitute the scandal of Christian dogma. A revolt against dogma, accordingly, and the substitution for it of an undogmatic Gospel is, plainly, a revolt against the Christianity of the New Testament.

Is it any wonder that our age has witnessed a bewildered pulpit? It is not easy to ignore two thirds of the New Testament or the faith of the Christian centuries.

Yet that is what, in effect, the modern pulpit has, partially at least, attempted. Are we now being asked to return to the prison house of scholastic theology? The prospect is a frightening one. Is there no way out? Have the results of the Enlightenment and of historicism, with their promise of release, no meaning? The question is one that is causing agony of conscience for many ministers. But hymnbooks and Bibles are still in our people's homes and in the pews of our churches. Can we unlock their mysteries once again for them and for ourselves—unexpurgated and trailing clouds of glory from the God of our fathers? Since the preacher may welcome even fumbling and inexpert help, the chapters that follow will attempt to show how we, in our time, can rediscover the power of dogmatic preaching.

CHAPTER II

Christ—Master or Saviour?

Analyses of the doubts about our modernist gospel that disturb us have been sketched thus far in briefest outline only. I cannot leave these doubts, however, without mention of a final one, which may serve as a kind of summary of those preceding.

As we go about our parishes, do we not, in moments of brutal honesty, ask ourselves questions about the final results of our sermons? We marvel again and again at the ocean of Christian grace that surrounds us. There are saints in our flocks, we observe, who put our discipleship to shame. Whence did they derive their power? Did it come to them from our preaching, or must we trace it to the liturgies in which they participate, to the hymns which they sing, and to the unexpurgated Bible which they read—all these still anchored in the dogmatic Christianity of their fathers and grandfathers? The thought surely gives us pause.

Is the Law Good News?

For, if we should be forced to find a theological category for many, if not most, of our sermons—those, at least, that preach the perfectionist moralism of our "historic Jesus" Christianity—we should have to confess that the category would be law, not grace. We have been placing burdens upon our people. We have preached to them in the imperative, not the indicative mood. Our sermons are *ought* sermons. Discipleship, presented as unadorned demand for performance, is an *ought*, not an *is*. It is law, and not grace. It is command, and not Gospel. So too with the Sermon on the Mount and our moralized parables and even with the imitation of Christ (we *ought* to be like Jesus). If we pause to reflect, there can surely come to us memories of the half-forgotten theological texts of our Bible. We may, perhaps, open our concordances to the word "law" and stand in holy fear before it, for the Law comes to us in the thunders and lightnings of Sinai and is set forth for us in the preaching of inexorable doom by the Old Testament prophets. We may chance upon a chapter like Deuteronomy 28:

It shall come to pass, if thou wilt not hearken unto the voice of Jehovah thy God, to observe to do all his commandments . . . Cursed shalt thou be in the city, and cursed in the field. Cursed shall be the fruit of thy body, and the fruit of thy ground, the increase of thy cattle, and the young of thy flock. Cursed shalt thou be when thou comest in, and cursed when thou goest out.—Deut. 28:15-19, ASV

Is this what we are *really* preaching when we preach the Gospel as an imperative? We shrink from the fearsome implications of such texts. They belong to the brimstone and hell-fire theology of the revival preaching of former unenlightened generations! We turn for comfort to the New Testament, first of all, to the teachings of Jesus. There, surely, we shall find no such burdensome law-religion. Have we not assured our people over and over again of the difference between the new law of love as over against the old law of threat and doom? But, if we read the Evangelists honestly, we get little relief. Even our beloved Sermon on the Mount can bring us to book with startling words:

Think not that I came to destroy the law or the prophets: I came not to destroy but to fulfill. For verily I say unto you, Till heaven and earth pass away, one jot or one tittle shall in no wise pass away from the law, till all things be accomplished. Whosoever therefore shall break one of these least commandments, and shall teach men so, shall be called least in the kingdom of heaven.—Matt. 5:17-19

The entire Sermon on the Mount, if interpreted in the light of this introduction, reads as if Jesus not only subscribed to Deuteronomy but even heightened the severity of the still relatively mild and external demands of the Mosaic moral code. And the sanctions that enforce this heightened law, like those behind the Mosaic law which preceded it, are inexorable sanctions. They are the fire and brimstone sanctions of our biblicist pulpit forefathers. "The Son of man will send his angels, and they will gather out of his kingdom all causes of sin and evil-doers, and throw them into the furnace of fire; there shall be weeping and gnashing of teeth" (Matt. 13:41,42, RSV).[a]

The Ought and If Only Sermon

We may well ask ourselves the disturbing question: If our preaching of the *oughts* and *we musts* of the Christian life is law-preaching, what are the sanctions which *we* have preached to enforce obedience? Can we trust to mere portrayals of the beauty and desirability of righteousness? Have we romanticised the demands of God and placed them in a land of dreams? Some of our sermons have been *if only* sermons: "If only all men would live by the ethics of the Sermon on the Mount or by the example of Jesus, all would be well with our sinful world. Let us, accordingly, at least make a beginning." But even the most moving vision of a utopian kingdom of God on earth is, as a sanction enforcing performance, a poor substitute for the "danger of hell-fire," threatened in the Sermon on the Mount, or the fear of Him "who, after he has killed, has power to cast into hell" (Luke 12:5, RSV). Since fear, as a motive for ac-

[a] Sources listed RSV are from the *Revised Standard Version of the Bible*. Copyrighted 1946 and 1952.

tion, may not be the highest of motives, we are prone to use texts like: "Perfect love driveth out fear." But "perfect love" is not produced by simple means either. Fear —Isaiah's dread cry, "Woe is me, for I am undone"— may be a necessary stage in bringing us to accept the good news of divine love. Like the Law that produces it, fear may be a schoolmaster to bring us to Christ.

If all we can present by way of sanction, in our homiletic exhortations, for the perfectionist ethic of the New Testament is the appeal of example and the innate urge to the good life in the human heart, we may be trusting a broken reed. What if the appeal fails, or is accepted merely as a beautiful romantic vision, or is even met with rebellion or with the secularist's realistic scorn, or, most importantly of all, is overwhelmed by the demonic powers of evil, what *then* is our recourse? We can only exhort in a higher key or portray the *we ought* of discipleship in more alluring colors. And if this still does not succeed, as it plainly does not with the alcoholics in our flock and the moral shipwrecks and those beaten down by tragedy and fate, what next?

Our tracing of the concept of law in the Bible has, I have suggested, come upon the "hard sayings" of Jesus. We can follow the guidance of our concordances further and enter the profound thought-world of St. Paul. Here we cannot escape "theology," though it be as yet an unsystematic theology and one which does not shout the word "dogma." Here the Gospel, however, becomes something more than an exhortation to live the good life. But a thoroughly critical reading of the sayings of Jesus, with the law-theology of the Old Testament as a guide, has made it clear that there is at least *latent* dogmatic theology even in the teachings of the Master. Dig deep enough, and it almost seems as if Jesus had studied the Epistles of St. Paul and had merely, with incomparable insight—a gift denied, alas, to St. Paul—translated theology into parables and practical sermons.

Be this as it may, the Law meets us in St. Paul's epistles in the form of a startling paradox. The Law is not abolished. It stands majestic and supreme, its sanctions still those of Deuteronomy and of the Last Judgment. It is as if St. Paul had before him as he wrote (as he well may have had) the very words of Jesus: "Till heaven and earth pass away, one jot or one tittle shall in no wise pass away from the law" (Matt. 5:18, ASV). Similarly St. Paul: "The law is holy, and the commandment holy, and righteous, and good" (Rom. 7:12, ASV). "We shall all stand before the judgment-seat of Christ" (Rom. 14:10), "We must all be made manifest before the judgment-seat of Christ; that each one may receive the things done in the body, according to what he hath done, whether it be good or bad" (II Cor. 5:10, ASV). Even immortality or a bodily resurrection will not save from judgment under the inexorable Law, for there "shall be a *resurrection* of the dead, both of the just *and unjust*" (Acts 24:15).

But St. Paul draws the inevitable conclusion. This Law, revealed in the conscience of the pagan, and then voiced by the God of the Old Testament, with threat of doom for those who disobey it, and finally revealed in the form of climactic demands in the person and teachings of Jesus, *will not save*. It is the very opposite of good news, though needful as preparing us for the Good News. It leads to death, not life. It kills. In his seventh chapter of The Epistle to the Romans, St. Paul relates his own experience of trying to live by law-religion: "I was once alive apart from the law, but when the commandment came, sin revived and I died; the very commandment which promised life proved to be death to me. For sin, finding opportunity in the commandment, deceived me and by it killed me" (Rom. 7:9-11).

St. Paul, we happily recall, does not stop with a portrayal of death as the end of the Law. He proclaims the Good News of Resurrection. But for a Gospel of Resurrection he needs a Christ other than an isolated Jesus of the Sermon on the Mount. This Christ will be the same historic Jesus, but now crucified and risen from the grave, at one and the same time Judge and Saviour, worshiped as Lord and God. He is a "now" Christ, not a "then" Christ. He is a contemporary Christ, and not merely a rabbi by the name of Jesus, whom we remember. No other Christ will, so St. Paul would tell us, do us any final good. Jesus, in the New Testament story, after the Resurrection, is no longer called Master. He is given a new name, equivalent to that of Deity, "far above all rule, and authority, and power, and dominion, and every name that is named, not only in this world, but also in that which is to come" (Eph. 1:21, asv).

Preach Jesus merely as the Master of a perfectionist ethics, so St. Paul might warn us modern preachers, and you may be preaching a gospel of death. Jesus remains then—what, indeed, He was—the climax of the Law. We shall not be able to endure Him. We shall have made of Him, as Luther devastatingly observes, "a task-master harder than Moses." Law, let us remind ourselves again, according to St. Paul, *kills*. Christ as revelation and climax of the Law will demand a dying on our part, or will Himself be crucified. This happened once, but it can, in a real sense, happen again and again. Are we, in preaching Christ as Law— granted that we conceal the awesome concept of law under the appealing words imitation and discipleship —tempting our listeners to crucify their Lord?

The Heresy of Idealism

The conclusion is too startling to be accepted without protest. Nor is it fair to our intentions. We could assert, for example, that bringing Deuteronomy and St. Paul and the teachings of biblical theology on law and grace into the argument is subjecting our discipleship preaching to precisely the dogmatic Christianity which we had laid aside at the outset. We admit that we have not preached the ethics of Jesus or the call to imitation and discipleship under the category of Deuteronomic law or of St. Paul's death-and-resurrection paradoxes.

We have been preaching the call to Christian moral heroism as an ideal, not as law.

Very well. But are we aware of what this means? The word "ideal" is not in the Bible. Nor is idealism a truly biblical category. In preaching the Gospel as an ideal, we may have stepped out of the Bible altogether, despite the fact that we have used texts out of the New Testament and have lyricized every paragraph by allusions to Jesus. By anthologizing our Bibles and aiming at an undogmatic gospel, we may have been preaching a new religion unknown to the Apostles or to the Church, Catholic and Protestant, until the last hundred years. Classical dogmatic Christianity may, of course, have been wrong. The Bible itself may have been mistaken. But if we are preaching a new gospel, we ought at least to know what we are doing. In expurgating our New Testaments, we have truly made a fateful decision.

The foregoing analysis has, admittedly, called into court only one of the major categories of biblical theology—the Law. The Law is, of course, not all of the Bible. It is, as St. Paul describes it, only a "schoolmaster," or, as a revised translation has it, "our custodian until Christ came" (Gal. 3:24). But the concept of law is, quite possibly, the crucial issue. Transform law into ideals, and everything is changed.

Ideals are impersonal. Nor do they cease to be impersonal when they receive the sanction of the teachings of

Jesus, or even of His divine-human example, or the moving call to imitate His perfection. You cannot pray to ideals. Nor will they save the weak and the lost. They may be reinforced by all manner of exhortations and sanctions on the human plane, and yet fail to ensure performance. Nor does it help ultimately to derive them from the lips of Christ and then to give Him traditional orthodox titles of respect—Christ, Lord, Son of God. Even discipleship of Jesus as Master can still remain outside the true thought-world of the New Testament. Such discipleship was tried, but it did not produce Christians. It ended in "forsaking" and treachery and failure. "We trusted that it had been he which should have redeemed Israel" (Luke 24:21), so the band of disciples expressed their tragic disappointment in Jesus at the climax of His earthly career. He had, alas, *not* redeemed Israel—not as Master!

I realize that branding our modern cult of the "historic Jesus" as mere impersonal idealism will strike many a devotee as utterly unfair. They will reply, "We have Jesus, not alone as teacher, but as person. Loyalty to Him—and discipleship as well—goes far beyond devotion to an ethical code or an ethical ideal."

Since a full discussion here of the place occupied by the "historic Jesus" in our Christianity "without dogma" would carry us far afield, a brief analysis must suffice.

The Remembered Jesus

One may grant, at the outset, that this undogmatic Christianity, with its "historic Jesus," has one thing in common with its rival. It has a remembered Christ. The Christianity of St. Paul and of the early Church had in its Gospel this remembered Jesus also, though it did not make Him the center of it. What happens when a remembered Jesus is thus isolated? He ceases to be the living Christ of the Christian creeds, resurrected and ascended, reigning as Lord in heaven and coming to judge the quick and the dead. Hence a relationship with Him must be by way of memory alone. Is this possible? Yes, clearly, in a way. Remembered figures in history can become contemporary. George Washington is still, for Americans, the "Father of his Country"; Abraham Lincoln retains his hold on our loyalty through his words and example. So too, Jesus. Indeed, as supreme expression of the divine in human history, His hold on the imagination can assume ethically inspiring forms. He was, so a devotee of undogmatic Christianity would assert, the First Christian—model, exemplar, friend, and brother of His disciples in His lifetime, and, by way of memory, our contemporary friend and brother, as well. Even the word "Saviour," extracted, to be sure, from its context in later theological dogma, can be metaphorically employed in describing His place in history.

A generation ago, few New Testament scholars were more honored in the schools than Johannes Weiss. We may well listen to one of his summaries of faith in the "historic Jesus" as his generation interpreted that faith. He says of the remembered Jesus:

We value Him as the highest gift which God has bestowed upon mankind, and place Him over against us as He comes to us from the hand of God. Through Him God speaks to us. At the same time we look on Him as one like ourselves who lived His life in complete obedience and childlike trust, who bore an immeasurable burden of sorrow, and yet did not despair of His heavenly Father. We see in Him the author and perfecter of our faith in the sense that He exemplified a kinship with God, to which we also are called in most perfect wise, experienced the loftiest blessedness of communion with God, and achieved a lasting peace of soul. We feel ourselves to be members of the new spiritual community of which He became the first exemplar, having won His own soul.[1]

This, Johannes Weiss argues, is enough for Christian faith. The "dogmatic Christ" of "late" New Testament thought has become for the modern believer impossible, though this Christ can find a place in history as proof precisely of the personal grandeur of Jesus:

We can learn from all these faltering attempts to express in formulae the nature of Christ: how His personality must have exercised the overpowering effect of inspiring men to such faith and of rousing such fantasy. If today we can no

[1] Johannes Weiss, *Die Nachfolge Christi and die Predigt der Gegenwart* (Göttingen: Vardenhoeck und Ruprecht, 1895), p. 121 (my translation).

longer understand their Christology or make it our own, we are directed all the more strongly to the person of Jesus. To understand Him, to gain an impression of His personality, to permit Him to draw us into His own life with the Father—that is for us far more important than the discovery of a confession which can combine dogmatic correctness with historic truth.[2]

The personality of Jesus. Who will deny its power? The Christianity of the apostolic era did not belittle it. But a gulf of infinite depth divides the two Christianities. Extract an "historic Jesus" from the New Testament, if you think you can do so. Quarreling with historians as historians may be futile. We are driven, however, to examine the result. Can the memory of the perfection of a personality solve even one of life's basic problems—death, tragedy, pain, guilt? Can an *idea* bring a sinner into communion with holy Deity? Jesus, we may say, assures us of God's love? But He assured us of God's inexorable demands also. We are invited to enter, by way of memory of an example, into *His* oneness with the Father, *His* trust, *His* heroism as He mounts His Cross. But note: *we* are to do all this. We are, in the final analysis, to be our own saviours, on the model of a First Christian, a remembered Companion. We are to win our own souls as He once won His. But this Jesus who is to do all this for us is to remain a mere Christ of past history, not the living Power of apostolic

---

[2] Weiss, *Die Anfänge des Dogmas* (Tübingen: Verlag von J. C. B. Mohr, 1909), p. 88 (my translation). Used by permission of the publisher.

faith. The Gospel turns, after all, into the presentation of an ideal—a personalized ideal, one may grant, but one with no sanctions of enforcement except our frail human wills. Apply to it, even for a moment, one of the true biblical categories, and it is seen to be a Gospel of "salvation by works alone." The Synoptic Gospels themselves contain, as pointed out earlier, the record of the failure of this "imitation of Jesus" religion. The disciples remained puzzled and defeated Jews until the later events of the drama of redemption had burst upon the historic scene.

Jesus as Offense

A complete presentation of the problems confronting the preacher of the Gospel, if he has been lured into loyalty to the undogmatic "historic Jesus" cult, would involve a wrestling with further biblical concepts in addition to that of the Law. But this, I would maintain, is still crucial. The gospel of the personality of Jesus has not escaped this category any more than has the gospel of the Sermon on the Mount. Turn law into ideals, and you sentimentalize and sophisticate the whole of the biblical revelation—yes, even the teachings of Jesus. In the Bible, as already indicated, we do not meet ideals, but commandments—commandments of a holy and living God. The whole problem of biblical religion centers in our relationship with this God of holiness, the Author of the Law. Place Jesus as revealer of perfection under this category, and He, too, becomes law. This is precisely one of the categories under which Christian faith accepted Him. He was in His person the holiness of the Word of God "made flesh." One has merely to read the New Testament itself, with unprejudiced eyes, to see written large a further conclusion. As incarnation of law, Jesus did not save. He laid bare the gulf between sinful man and the holy God to the point where men could not endure Him. Precisely the religious man, the Jew of proud law-religion, crucified this Jesus. Bring Him back by way of sentimental remembrance today, will He not once more become an offense? Confronted by Him, we may again cry for the Christ of faith, the Saviour Christ of St. Paul, the Christ of the Cross and the Resurrection, the Christ of "theology."

Who of us today can boast that he has been guiltless of turning the glorious Gospel of the New Testament into an ethical self-salvation cult? We have all been deceived—at least, in part. The historians have played us false. Our expurgated Bibles are an embarrassment on our shelves. We have been laying burdens on the weary shoulders of our people. We have sentimentalized the Law and called it an ideal. We have reduced Christ from God to human prophet and moral hero. We have preached discipleship and the imitation of Jesus, not realizing that this, too, when isolated from the Good News of the Cross and the Resurrection, is burden, and *not* Good News. Where are our parishioners and we ourselves to get the strength to fulfill all this *oughtness?* *Oughtness* is, plainly, not the Good News. Ideals do not command nor save. Even a remembered Jesus, if He is nothing more than this, lacks powers to command or save. It takes a God, with doom and salvation under His control, to move the stubborn will of man, to humble pride, and to bring us into a personal interview with the "Maker of heaven and earth and Judge of all men."

To transform the preaching of the ideals of the Christian life from *oughtness* to *isness* will mean a revolution in many a pulpit and homiletic workshop. It will mean a return to an unexpurgated Bible. It will mean a return to *theology.* In my wrestling with our modernist gospel thus far, I have, as already indicated, brought onto the stage of the argument only one of the major categories of the Bible—the Law. The Good News category of Grace awaits an entrance cue in the wings. But the biblical category of the Law suffices to illustrate the difference between preaching our ethical idealism as an *ought* and presenting it as an *is.* Turn once more to Deuteronomy. The Law does not meet us there as a mere *ought.* The Law in Deuteronomy is an *is.* Obedience *is* blessedness; disobedience *is* doom. Predictions about the outcome are voiced as calmly and inexorably as are those of a scientist who announces a tested formula in chemistry or physics.

Law and grace, and the other key concepts of biblical religion, such as sin, forgiveness, justification, salvation, and many more, are not primarily ethical or moral categories at all. No secular textbook on ethics will discuss them, though it may deal with ethical idealism on every page and match our supposedly Christian vision of "the good life" almost word for word, not excluding an ethical hero-portrait of Jesus. Bible ethics is theological ethics. It involves a relationship with a personal and holy God, and the solution of problems prior to all problems of conduct. Even the Ten Commandments are not mere *oughtness,* nor are they examples of moral idealism. The Ten Commandments appear in the biblical record as part of a drama of grace and salvation, and in a context of person-to-person relationship. They exemplify an ethic of response to an *is,* not an ethic of response to a utopian ideal. "I am the Lord thy God which have brought thee out of Egypt, out of the house of bondage." *Therefore,* "Thou shalt have no other gods before me." *Therefore,* "Thou shalt not steal." *Therefore, . . .*

The word "therefore," expressed or implied, marks the gulf between all ethical moralism as mere *oughtness* and the moral demands of biblical faith. It appears boldly underscored in the ethics of the New Testament. St. Paul's moral exhortations make sense only when preceded by St. Paul's theology. Eleven chapters of his Epistle to the Romans deal with theology. Only then does he introduce the subject of Christian ethics. His twelfth chapter opens with the words: "I beseech you, *therefore,* brethren, by the mercies of God, to present your bodies as a living sacrifice . . ." (Rom. 12:1, ASV).

Back to Dogma

Enough may now have been said to arouse us to severe self-examination as we preach our undogmatic New Testament texts and our moralizing Gospel. Back we must go, even in our practical sermons and our simple talks to lay people, to once despised dogmatics, to a theological Bible, to a Christ of the Creeds, as well as to the Christ of historians.

Indictments of our moralistic pulpit, at any rate, are appearing today on many fronts. I call to witness a few ringing confessions of our corporate guilt. One of our contemporaries describes our dangerous state thus:

We moderns have made a great mistake in our ethical interpretation of Christianity. Jesus, we have said, showed us in His life and teachings the true way of life. The Church, so again we have said, exists for the admirable purpose of realizing Jesus' moral ideals. This conception of the Church I must emphatically disavow. I regard it as a grave, if not a terrible mistake. To conceive the Christian Church as resting upon an ethical basis is to sacrifice the substance of the Christian faith. The ultimate thing about Christianity is not its ethics, but its ontology. The basic affirmations are not concerning what *ought* to be, but concerning what *is* . . .[3]

[3] Quoted by permission from a personal letter from a colleague who confesses that he cannot recall the source.

The contrast between *ought* and *is,* in this confession, can remind us of a saying of which Baron Friedrich von Hügel was especially fond: "No amount of *Oughtness* can be made to take the place of *Isness.*" [4]

Or, to cite a second warning—one in which a gospel of *oughtness* is once more confronted by the true *isness* of Good News:

The Gospel is not an imperative; it is an indicative. The imperative which we have in our own conscience does not give the strength to do what we ought to do. If the Gospel consisted in an ideal and in demands, it would not be an *Eu-angelion* but a *Dys-angelion,* that is—sad tidings. It is an *Eu-angelion* because the first thing it does is not to demand but to give. It gives to the World what the World neither has nor knows; it discloses the secret of God's loving purpose, the message of reconciliation; thus laying a foundation for community.[5]

And if we should be tempted to retort that our preaching does not limit itself to a presentation of ethical precepts, but, instead, presents the appeal of a person, the Jesus of history Himself, our theologians will not leave us at ease there either. Contemporary New Testament scholarship comes to their aid. As is now well known, a revolution occurred in the schools as a result of Albert Schweitzer's disturbing book, *The*

[4] Cited in a passage, in which this theme receives further wise treatment, in A. E. Taylor's *The Faith of a Moralist* (London: The Macmillan Co., 1932), II, p. 136.
[5] Emil Brunner, *The Word and the World* (New York: Charles Scribner's Sons, 1931), p. 125. Used by permission of the publisher.

Quest of the Historical Jesus, and the rise of what is now technically known as *Formgeschichte.* It is becoming increasingly clear that the biography of Jesus, historically reconstructed as a "Life of Jesus Christ," and then made the foundation for an undogmatic Christianity, is a romantic fiction. A. E. Taylor, whose *Faith of a Moralist* is one of the most masterly guides in leading us back to a theological evaluation of biblical evidence, is only one voice in a chorus when he says:

We are bound in honesty, I think, even from the point of view of the most judiciously conservative criticism, to admit that we really know much less about the Master's life than might be supposed at first sight, or than we could wish. It is not too much to say that there never has been, and never will be, a trustworthy *Life of Jesus Christ;* we have no materials for such a work outside the Gospels, and the purpose of the Evangelists was not that of a biographer.[6]

The author underscores the fact that for the early Christians the significance of Christ consisted in the new life "in Christ," which Jesus had left as a legacy after His resurrection and the sending of the Pentecostal Spirit.

They did not infer the transcendent significance of Christ from an antecedent belief in the moral perfection of his character, or the ethical elevation of his recorded sayings: rather they inferred these—though it is significant how little appeal any of the New Testament writings outside

[6] A. E. Taylor, *The Faith of a Moralist* (London: The Macmillan Co., 1932), II, p. 128. Used by permission of the publisher.

the Synoptic Gospels make to ethical precepts of Jesus—
from their antecedent belief in the transcendent significance of Christ as the 'glorified' sender of the Spirit. *And
one may fairly doubt whether, in later days, any man has
ever really been converted to the Christian faith simply by
the impression made on him either by the story of Christ's
life or by the reports of his moral teachings.*[7]

The riddle of the New Testament, as it has come to
be called, may deserve much further investigation and
may not be resolved in favor of dogmatic orthodoxy as
easily as the above quotation asserts. The "historic
Jesus" must retain His place in the drama of Redemption. He is not merely God "veiled" in the flesh, as Bar-
thian theology seems to assert, but God "unveiled."
Kierkegaard's striking words are only partial truth when
he says: "If the contemporary generation had left behind them nothing but the words, 'we have believed
that in such and such a year God appeared among us
in the humble figure of a servant, that He lived and
taught in our community, and finally died,' it would
be more than enough." [8] One could call to Kierkegaard's
attention the fact that the holiness of God "in the flesh"
is revelation, as well as is the Cross and the Resurrection. (Kierkegaard, indeed, in other of his writings,
makes much of the humanity of the God-Man.)

[7] *Ibid.*, pp. 129-30. The italics are mine.
[8] Soren Kierkegaard, *Philosophical Fragments* (Princeton University Press, 1936), p. 87.

The "Dogmatic" Life of Christ

Nevertheless, the contemporary protest against the "Jesus of history" Christianity has, in its turn, right on its side. Only when the story of the Prophet of Nazareth—important as one act in the drama—is seen in the perspective of a cosmic action in which God "for us and for our salvation came *down* from heaven," can it have any ultimate significance. To isolate that life and to make it central for the Gospel is to write a new gospel undreamed of by either the Apostles or the Evangelists.[9]

Hence the dilemma which the modern preacher faces, in deciding between a dogmatic and an undogmatic Christ, remains acute. Both pulpit and Sunday school classroom have unquestionably dealt with the life of Christ—the biography, that is, of Jesus of Nazareth from birth to death—as somehow the center of the

[9] One of the best discussions of this "Riddle of the New Testament," is the volume bearing this title by Hoskyns and Davies (London: Faber and Faber, 1936). Another wise attempt to reinstate the "Jesus of history" in contemporary theological thought is to be found in D. M. Baillie's *God Was in Christ* (New York: Charles Scribner's Sons, 1948), pp. 30-54. Baillie summarizes there the current debate, in which Karl Barth is, of course, a prominent figure.

A true solution of the riddle, I venture to suggest, may be found when we wrestle further with the dialectic between Law and Grace. The Word "made flesh" was a revelation of *both* the holiness *and* mercy of God. Without the teachings of the "historic Jesus" serving as necessary "schoolmaster," the Gospel of the Cross and Resurrection would have been sentimental or "cheap" grace.

Gospel. The very word "Gospel" has come to be synonymous with the plural form, the Gospels. This biography of Jesus, so we have long accustomed ourselves to think, simply must be primary. St. Paul's theological biography of Jesus, or, in fact, that of the early Church's proclamation generally, is for us commentary, not original text. Even when we are not consciously trying to place Jesus over against St. Paul, as in the Jesus *or* Paul formula, we find it almost impossible to see the life of Christ in the same way the New Testament, as a whole, actually presents it and as it must have been viewed even by the Evangelists. Until we recapture the New Testament version, however, we shall never face up honestly to the challenge which the rediscovered biblical theology of our generation forces upon us and which we cannot, in panic or cowardice, really escape. It is possible that we shall have to face the apparent dilemma "Jesus *or* Paul," discovering at the same time that voting for Jesus as against St. Paul is not only untheological Christianity, but unhistorical Christianity as well—a realization that can be embarrassing in many pulpits.

How far our "life of Christ" Gospel differs from what the New Testament Christians meant by the phrase (St. Paul uses it freely) can be vividly documented by recent New Testament scholarship. A competent contemporary Pauline authority boldly states this:

The words "the life of Christ" mean for us the career of Jesus of Nazareth, but for Paul they would have meant something quite different—the present reality and lordship of the risen one. So, indeed, he actually uses an equivalent phrase in Romans 5:10: "For if, while we were enemies we were reconciled to God by the death of his Son, much more, now that we are reconciled, shall we be saved by his life." The "life of Christ" is, not the remembered life that preceded his death, but the life which followed it—the present life of the Son of God . . . When *we* read the phrase "Christ and him crucified," we think first of the human Jesus, of his life of devotion and service, and our minds move forward to the cross; but when Paul wrote the phrase, he was thinking first of all of the risen, exalted Christ, and his thought moved *backward* to the cross. Perhaps this fact partly explains the paucity of allusions to Jesus' earthly life in Paul's letters. His attention, as it moves backward, is arrested by the Crucifixion, which itself epitomizes so perfectly the theological significance and the moral character of the whole earthly life that he does not look beyond it; having begun, so to speak, from the end of the book, he has already reached the climax of the story.[10]

The "life of Christ" of the New Testament faith did not ignore the career of Jesus, the rabbi of Nazareth, to any such extent as the apparent contrast "Jesus *or* Paul" would indicate. Proof of this lies in the utterly simple fact that this same apostolic Church wrote the Gospels. *Formgeschichte*, whatever may be its final value, has at least taught us one thing. The Evangelists lived as members of the early Church, and wrote within the context of that Church's faith. They were theologians. When we moderns appeal to a "historic Christ" in con-

[10] John Knox, *Chapters in a Life of Paul* (Nashville: Abingdon Press, 1950), pp. 130-31. Used by permission of the publisher.

trast to the Christ of dogma, we are, of all things, precisely unhistorical.

Christ as Ascended Lord

A quite defensible paradox, though one which is admittedly violent, could be the following: That the phrase "the historic Christ," like the phrase "the life of Christ" ought, in loyalty to New Testament faith, to connote the risen and ascended Lord in place of the life of Jesus before His resurrection. "Historic in what sense?" is a proper question to ask. "Historic *now*," "in history *now*," would be the answer of classical Christianity. "Historic once in the past," "historic *then*," might be the answer of modern historicism. The paradox, in its true New Testament version, need not in the least belittle the "historic" narrative of the Gospels. In a drama, you cannot have a fourth act without a preceding third act, or second, or first. The phrase "suffered under Pontius Pilate" is permanently anchored in the Creeds. But neither the Bible nor Christian faith is interested in museum history. Salvation is always a present or a future, as well as a past, event. Salvation is an eschatological fact or hope, even when it is already "realized eschatology" and, therefore, present as well as future. One utterly simple explanation of the time-puzzle in the New Testament is that the apostolic age was unashamedly "modern." It was contemporary and realistic, not romantic. It sang no sentimental hymns to

Jesus. It dealt with Him, not in memory only or in the past tense, but as a living Power in the present and as coming Judge. "I am the first and the last, and the *living* one; I *was* dead; and, behold, I *am alive* for evermore, and *have* the keys of hell and of death" (Rev. 1:17-18, AV and ASV). Jesus had once acted out His heavenly Father's will in the reigns of Herod and Pilate, but He is now ascended and, as the Apostles' Creed declares, is "sitting at the right hand of God."

It was precisely this Christ, risen and ascended, who was Lord for the Apostolic Church. This present Lordship in no way denied the importance of the story before the Resurrection and the Ascension. There would have been no drama of salvation, of a divine descent, and of a rising again, no atonement, no covenant of reconciliation, no good news of any kind *without* the humiliation and coming *down* of the Son of God. When St. Paul summarizes his Gospel, he regularly underscores phrases like "made of the seed of David according to the flesh," or "taking the form of a slave" and "made in the likeness of man" (Rom. 1:3; Phil. 2:6,7, RSV). But the Gospel was not limited to this earlier act of the drama. The Gospel is the drama's climax and its result —the Cross and the new life "in Christ" for which alone the Word had become "flesh" and for which the Son of God had "emptied himself" and "dwelt among us" (Phil. 2:7; John 1:14).

To see further how revolutionary for our preaching a re-enthronement of the biblical theologian and consequent dethronement of the undogmatic historian can be, I cite another contemporary witness—Peter Taylor Forsyth. Few men, in the generation when the cult of "the historic Jesus" held almost undisputed sway, predicted so clearly the debacle of authentic Christian faith to which such a displacement of authority would lead. I am tempted to fill pages with citations of his epigrams and "winged words"—particularly from his masterpiece, *The Person and Place of Jesus Christ,* or his Yale lectures on preaching, *Positive Preaching and the Modern Mind.*[11]

A few citations must suffice. The major flaw in the schools of his day and in the stress of the preaching that they fostered, he locates in the modern attempt to anchor faith in the synoptic life of Jesus in place of the dogmatic Christ of the New Testament as a whole. "If we keep critically to the Synoptics, can the Christ of the New Testament be retained?" "Undogmatic Christianity repudiates the New Testament interpretation of Christ." "It may be asked whether the Synoptic Christ, when read without the medium of the epistles, could have floated Christianity out into the world."[12]

Forsyth goes even further and ranks the epistles of the New Testament, in their importance for our anchorage in apostolic faith, definitely above the Gospels:

[11] Both volumes (dated originally 1909 and 1907 respectively) have recently been republished (1949) by the Independent Press, Memorial Hall, London.

[12] P. T. Forsyth, *The Person and Place of Jesus Christ* (London: Independent Press, 1949), pp. 104 and 175. Used by permission of the publisher.

The Epistles are more inspired than the Gospels. We are in more direct contact with Christ. We are at one remove only. The Gospels, with their unspeakable value, are yet propaedeutic to the Epistles; and most of the higher pains and troubles of the Church today arise from the displacement of its center of gravity to the Gospels.[13]

Our Modernist Heresy

These are, for our generation, disturbing words. Yet a glimpse backward through Christian history will surely validate them. Even the historical liturgies of the Church preserve the custom of reading the Gospel for the day *after* the reading of the Epistle. Only through the eyes of the Church's *preached* Gospel can the *historic* Gospel story receive its rightful meaning.

On Christianity as ethical idealism and imitation of Jesus, Forsyth utters equally important warnings: "A lofty ideal is not mighty to save." An honest reading of the New Testament record of the early Christians will lead to the conviction that "as far back as we can go, we find only the belief and worship of a risen, redeeming, and glorified Christ, whom they could wholly trust, but only very poorly imitate; and in his relation to God could not imitate at all." Two Christianities confront each other in the modern Church: "For the one Christ is the object of our faith, for the other he is the captain of our faith, its greatest instance. In the one case we

[13] Forsyth, *Theology in Church and State* (London: Independent Press, 1949), p. 31. Used by permission of the publisher.

believe *in* Christ, in the other we believe *like* Christ. In the one we trust our whole selves to Christ for ever, in the other we imitate him. In the one he is our God, in the other our brother. It is well that the issue should be clear." [14]

In view of the rise of our modernist Christianity of ideals, so Forsyth can climax his analysis, all past schisms in Christian history pale into relative insignificance. Even the gulf between Rome and Protestantism is not half so serious. The Reformation movement turned on "the matter of sin, repentance, confession and absolution." But this did not mean the rise of a new Christianity. The Reformation underscored what had always been "a central affair of Christianity—a religion of repentance and forgiveness. Roman, Greek and Protestant Christianity are here at one. And the declaration now that Christianity consists in imitating, at a reverent distance, the religion of Jesus only shows that we are in the midst of a movement and an apostasy more serious than anything that has occurred in the Church's history since Gnosticism was overcome." [15]

I shall not follow Forsyth's incisive criticism of modernist Christianity further, though his writings can be recommended as furnishing a clear picture of our contemporary strife of tongues. I venture to place on the witness stand, instead, one more champion of a return

[14] Forsyth, *The Person and Place of Jesus Christ*, pp. 73, 44, 189-90. Used by permission of the publisher.
[15] Forsyth, *The Person and Place of Jesus Christ*, pp. 51-2.

to dogmatic and biblical orthodoxy—one who again sees our present dilemma as consisting in the choice we have to make between preaching a "biography of Jesus" or preaching the "dogma" of apostolic faith. This writer asks:

What then is the object of Christian faith? Not a man who once lived and died, but a Contemporary Reality, a God whose awful holiness is "covered" by one who is both our representative and his, so that it is our flesh that we see in the Godhead, that "flesh" which was historically Jesus of Nazareth, but is eternally the divine Christ whose disclosure and apprehension Jesus lived and died to make possible.[16]

The Christian faith, so the author continues, rests upon more than the life of Jesus between Bethlehem and Calvary. This life, in fact, is but part of a much larger whole—the drama of the Incarnation and Atonement that leads to a doctrine of the Trinity. Why do we moderns rebel against this "theological" Christianity? The real reason lies deep. It is human pride:

We would fain be self-sufficient and this means we are not. We would fain be masters of our fate and the captains of our souls, and this says that our fate is in another's hands and that our souls have been bought with a price.

In a paragraph that is as frank as indictment of our perilous state as I have met anywhere in contemporary theological writing, the author concludes:

[16] Edwin Lewis, "The Fatal Apostasy of the Modern Church," in *Religion in Life* (Autumn, 1933), p. 487. Used by permission of the publisher.

But in this pride lies our shame, our weakness and our defeat. What has it done for us? What has it done for the Church—at least for evangelical Protestantism? How far have we gotten with our various substitutes? Look over our churches: They are full of people, who, brought up on these substitutes, are strangers to those deeper experiences without which there had been no New Testament and no Church of Christ. Thousands of clergymen will go into their pulpits next Sunday morning, but not as prophets. There will be no burning fire shut up in their bones, by reason of which they cannot forbear to speak. . . . Grievous is the hurt of the daughter of God's people, and slight is the proffered healing. They go to Gilead, there is no balm. They go to the fountain of waters, and they find there a broken cistern. They cry for bread, and behold a stone.[17]

[17] Lewis, pp. 488-9.

CHAPTER III

A Clue to Biblical Theology

Enough has been said in the previous chapters, I trust, to prove that we are in the midst of a theological revival that challenges the contemporary pulpit. Each one of us will have to answer for himself to what extent he is being called upon to submit to a searching of conscience and to a fresh encounter with the Church's historic faith. But I am convinced that I speak for hundreds of my brethren in the ministry when I confess that our mood must be one of penitence and of standing under judgment. The escape from the strait jacket of creeds and dogmas—an escape that once seemed glorious—has proved to be an illusion. Back we must go to theology.

The Road Back to Theology

But the road back to theology is not going to be easy traveling. We are preachers and pastors, not doctors of divinity even when that title appears after our names on parish bulletin boards. The age-old gulf between practical sermon and theological textbooks still remains. We cannot possibly satisfy the demand for a return to a dogmatic Christianity simply by preaching the technical doctrinal systems of the schools or by transforming our sermon hours (which are often only quarter hours, anyway) into amateurish seminary lectures. Even our denominational confessions cannot be nakedly brought into the pulpit. Here are two samples from one of the briefest of these confessions, the Thirty-nine Articles of Anglicanism:

Original sin standeth not in the following of Adam (as the Pelagians do vainly talk;) but it is the fault and corruption of the Nature of every man, that naturally is engendered of the offspring of Adam; whereby man is very far gone from original righteousness, and is of his own nature inclined to evil, so that the flesh lusteth always contrary to the Spirit; and therefore in every person born into this world, it deserveth God's wrath and damnation. And this infection of nature doth remain, yea in them that are regenerated; whereby the lust of the flesh . . . is not subject to the Law of God. And although there is no condemnation for them that believe and are baptized; yet the Apostle doth confess, that concupiscence and lust hath of itself the nature of sin. (Article IX.)

Predestination to Life is the everlasting purpose of God, whereby (before the foundations of the world were laid) he hath constantly decreed by his counsel secret to us, to deliver from curse and damnation those whom he hath chosen in Christ out of mankind, and to bring them by Christ to everlasting salvation, as vessels made to honour. Wherefore, they which be endued with so excellent a benefit of God, be called according to God's purpose by his Spirit working in due season; they through grace obey the calling: they be justified freely: they be made sons of God by adoption: they be made like the image of his only-begotten Son Jesus Christ: they walk religiously in good works, and at length, by God's mercy, they attain to everlasting felicity. (Article XVII, in part.)

It seems a far cry from the days when laymen, as well as clergy and the doctors of the schools, were exercised over the niceties of these doctrinal formulae and when the turn of a phrase could mark the dividing line between Christian communions. The Queen of the sciences has large territories of illiteracy to recover before her recaptured reign will again be secure. Our neo-theological era, as a matter of fact, is raising from the dead issue after issue of the doctrinal debates of past centuries, and rightly so. As the divisions of Christendom were once caused by a theological warfare of conviction, so the reunion of the churches involves tracing these clashing loyalties back to their source.

One need merely think, by way of example, of the battles that once raged around the doctrine of predestination or the doctrine of justification by faith, which latter became the battle cry of the Reformation. A recent observer of our contemporary scene says of this doctrine:

It is so strange to the modern man that there is scarcely any way of making it intelligible to him. And yet this doctrine of justification by faith has divided the old unity of

Christendom; has torn asunder Europe, and especially Germany; has made innumerable martyrs; has kindled the bloodiest and most terrible wars of the past; and has deeply affected European history and with it the history of humanity. This whole complex of ideas which for more than a century—not so very long ago—was discussed in every household and workshop, in every market and country inn . . . is now scarcely understandable even to our most intelligent scholars. We have here a breaking down of tradition that has few parallels.[1]

Must those of us who are being shamed into a return to theology overleap the centuries and go back to all this doctrinal warfare? Will it not threaten the emerging unification of our long alienated churches? Can we, even with the best will in the world, interest our laity once again in doctrinal matters that are today as foreign to them as the mathematical mysteries of Einstein? We may as well face the issue. Our reborn theological era will not let us alone. In one sense we shall have to go back to our dust-covered volumes on divinity, as well as to those of our contemporary doctors. Theology is serious business, and has been since the days of St. Paul. Preaching the Gospel is serious business. The fact that, in the long history of the Church, insights into the Gospel have got themselves tangled up in a technical vocabulary is not evidence that the insights are not valid or important. Soldiers in battle are not experts in

[1] Paul Tillich, *The Protestant Era* (The University of Chicago Press, 1948), p. 196. Copyright 1948 by the University of Chicago. Used by permission of the publisher.

engineering, but their very lives depend upon the technicalities of drafting boards, the science of ballistics, and the precision of laboratory apparatus. The eternal salvation of our people, as the debacle of humanist Christianity proves, depends upon the agonized toilings of the Church's technical theologians. We must, perforce, leave to the doctors in the schools the toil of working out a relevant theology for our time, but we are in duty bound to make known from the pulpit their conclusions. Many of us are tempted to limit our professional reading to a few popular "helps for the clergy" (which some one has called "pithy points for played-out preachers"). In our days of crisis, this simply will not do. We are cheating ourselves and our people of the most thrilling token of grace that God is bestowing upon His Church in our generation—the dynamic rediscovery of the Catholic faith of Christendom. It is not an accident that the Church of South India, in which four variant traditions have found union, is discovering in a revival of basic Christian theology one of its most significant sources of power.

A Promise of Freedom

Yet, in my plea for a return of the contemporary pulpit to theology, I have overstated my case. Some bewilderment and apprehension, at least on the part of the humble preacher, is not without excuse. Good news is around the corner. We are not going to be called upon

to submit to the doctrinal orthodoxies of past centuries
—not, at any rate, in quite the form of an intellectual
strait jacket, such as once tyrannized our forefathers.
The Queen of the sciences is, indeed, back on her
throne, but a new dynasty has, as it were, taken over.
The historical study of the Bible once promised a complete release from her queenly rule. This was an illusion. Undogmatic Christianity has again been shown to
be no Christianity at all, but mere humanism covered
with a mantle of sentiment. Nevertheless, the long
reign of the historian over the theologian has left us a
priceless legacy of freedom.

This emancipation consists basically in one simple,
yet profound, rediscovery—the fact, namely, that God's
revelation of Himself to man was not given in the form
of truths and propositions to be logically tied together
in faultless systems of divinity, but in deeds, in "mighty
acts," in a story or drama.[2] The Bible is the record of
this revelation and man's acceptance of it—particularly
the acceptance of it by a people specifically chosen (pre-
destinated) by God to be the bearer of His Word to all
mankind. This substitution of a revelation given in
deeds for one manifested in truths or propositions does
not, of course, solve all problems. It does little more than
to shift theological effort from the task of building logical systems to that of penetrating the meaning and rele-

[2] One of the best brief accounts known to me of what this
insight into the true nature of revelation implies is the opening
chapter of Leonard Hodgson's *The Doctrine of the Trinity* (London: Nisbet & Co., 1943).

vancy of historical events. The reign of historicism in
the past century was, after all, not wholly on the wrong
track. It went astray only in limiting its acceptance of
historical events or facts to those events or facts in
which man was the actor. It became, in its extreme
forms, virtually a Christianity without God—a story of
religious man seeking the divine, rather than the story
of God finding man.

But historical events or stories, like masterpieces of
dramatic art, can receive varying or even antithetic in-
terpretations. We can, for example, call to mind what
literary criticism has done with Shakespeare's *Hamlet*.
A mild chaos of proposed clues to the meaning of the
play confronts the serious student. The "mighty acts"
recorded in the Bible also need interpretation; and the
theologian becomes the necessary intermediary. First of
all, we need the theology of the Bible itself—the
preached Gospel of the early Church, its *kerygma*, or
proclamation. We find this strewn broadcast through
our New Testaments. "The God of our fathers raised
up Jesus whom ye slew, hanging him on a tree. Him
did God exalt with his right hand to be a Prince and a
Saviour, to give repentance to Israel, and remission of
sins. And we are witnesses of these things, and so is the
Holy Spirit, whom God hath given to them that obey
him" (Acts 5:31-32). Here is one of the earliest in-
stances of the newborn Gospel receiving formulation in
a sermon. Here is history, the kind of history that the
historian can deal with, but it is history *plus*. It is "the-

ologized" history, history seen through the eyes of a faith. God has entered into the "plot," as it were, as chief Actor in an action transcending the mere biography of a human being. Words like Prince, Saviour, Holy Spirit, repentance, and remission of sins now carry us into realms of meaning not limited to moral philosophy or to homiletic exhortations for a more noble way of living. Here is an *is*, first of all, not an *ought*.

As we read on in the New Testament, the clue to the action becomes clearer and clearer. In the biography of Jesus, if that is the right designation for the narrative central in the New Testament, faith sees more than a story about a human hero. It sees revelation of Deity— an action in which God enters into a new relationship with sinful man. History in the Bible becomes salvation-history, or redemption-history, or what, in the more vivid German expression, is called *Heilsgeschichte*. Even the purely human events in the story receive theological interpretation. Identify Jesus as Son of God— God in the flesh—and His person and His teachings literally do become theology. His person becomes Word of God, and His teachings become words of God.

Nevertheless, the rediscovery of biblical theology as story-theology does emancipate us from that tyranny of the intellect which the word "orthodoxy" still connotes in popular views of traditional Christianity. It is still theology—very clearly so—but a theology that need not submit to any particular system of divinity. Systems of divinity, seen in perspective, are necessary in the Church's ongoing life. But these fulfill their rightful function only insofar as they guard the Church's faith against losing the clue to the action-theology with which all started and on which all depends. The historic Creeds, which are crucial examples, have this guardian-ship *alone* as their aim. They were never designed as substitutes for the original revelation in deed and act. They simply summarize this revelation-story, making sure that the action is seen in proper cosmic perspective. Jesus must, in a "theological" version of the story, be accepted as actor in a drama of redemption in which God is the Saviour, and man a sinner requiring salva-tion. Some kind of identification between God and Christ is essential to this story. Ignore this key to the meaning of the action, and we could preach from the Bible till doomsday, and yet not preach the Christian Gospel.

And all later theological science in Christian history, including its awesome systems of divinity, its confessions and catechisms, should have had, as their proper aim, nothing beyond this protection of genuine biblical theology. They have proved to be a danger to the Church only when the Bible, in place of being seen as the record of revelation in act and deed, has been treated as a book containing revelation in the form of propositions that can be manipulated as figures are on a logical chessboard.

The Gospel Began as a Preached Gospel

The days of the literalist Bible, however, are numbered. As already indicated, the critical historians have freed us from that slavery. Our danger is the opposite one—to treat the Bible as if it contained no theology at all. We can thank our contemporary theologians for rescuing us, if we will permit them to do so, from this alternate pathway to destruction. We can thank them further for giving us a theology that is precisely biblical theology. The Bible on our pulpits can regain its rightful inheritance. It is lord even over the theology of the learned doctors. For biblical theology has rediscovered the fact that the Gospel began as a *preached* Gospel. The Gospel, in other words, began with sermons. The first theologians of the Church were preachers, not learned doctors of the schools.

Indeed, when our contemporary theologians have fulfilled their task as guardians of the Gospel and have given us back our unexpurgated Bibles, we, the preachers of the Church, can again be the Church's primary theologians. If the Gospel began as a preached Gospel, a preached Gospel it must remain, or lose its power. If God's revelation came to man in deed, and not in formalized propositions, its life among men must continue to exist primarily in deed, and only secondarily in propositional form. It is to us, the proclaimers of the Gospel to living men, the pastors of living souls, the priests of a living Church, that the ivory-tower theologian must look for the living insights that he is called upon to guard and to defend against the Church's enemies. The ultimate teacher in the Church is the Holy Spirit. The Spirit is the gift given to the Church as corporate Body of Christ. The learned scholar, the historian, the professor of dogmatics, stands under the judgment of the Spirit-bearing community, the Church. And we, the shepherds and ministers of the Church, are the primary bearers of the Church's power.

This paradox of the taught instructing their teachers may seem perverse and motivated by pride. Yet, surely, it is high time that the pulpit find the strength to cast off its sense of inferiority and that it assume once more its rightful place of authority in the Church—a Church which includes the Church's theologians. The stirring phrase "biblical theology," we can repeatedly remind ourselves, consists of two words. While it denotes theology, it connotes a recovered Bible. And who are they that live in closest contact with the Bible? Clearly, the Church's proclaimers of the Gospel. The Bible is enthroned on our pulpits. For us and our people, it is still *Holy* Scripture. Texts from it are for them, as for us, still sacred texts. We might be surprised to find how little the storms of the Enlightenment have really robbed the Bible of its ancient power over the hearts of our listeners. They, like ourselves, merely need to recapture the clue to its majestic drama. For if the Bible is the record of revelation in act and deed, our congregations, like ourselves, can rediscover the thrilling, though also awesome, fact that it is a drama not ended. The action is about us! We are members of the cast! Should the drama come alive again in our parish flocks and in our hearts, even the learned doctors would have to come to us to see its real meaning in action.

The Bible as Drama

The Bible a drama—a contemporary drama? Yes, this is the Bible that our theologians have given back to us. The rediscovery, fully utilized in pulpit and parish life, can mean the rebirth of a dynamic Church of Christ, unparalleled in history since the days of the Apostles. The Gospel, it almost seems, has been, for some generations at least, like a treasure hidden in a field. Once seen again as the treasure above price, we in our generation may again sell all that we have to repossess it.

And what is the clue to this our familiar and ever strange Bible? We wish to profit now from what our theologians have taught us: the Bible is revelation in act and deed, not in abstracted truths or propositions. Where can we begin? Surprisingly enough, the clue stares us in the face on the Bible's title page—possibly, the most neglected page of Holy Scripture.

THE HOLY BIBLE, Containing the Old and New Testaments—so reads its title. *Testament*. Does *this* word carry meaning any longer to the modern mind? Here, at the very outset, we need to make use of the art of translation—what has been called the art of "money-changing." [3] Very well; we translate. Testament, we say, means covenant. But, alas, this does not help us much. "Money-changing" is once more called for. The word "covenant," in turn, while more meaningful in our contemporary vocabulary than the word "testament," carries no thrill. Synonyms like "contract" or "bargain" are the best that come to mind. But these terms, alas, play directly into the hands of those who advocate that moralistic version of Christianity which has bedevilled our modernist era. According to their interpretation, a decent observance of the Golden Rule, admiration of Jesus as example, and a continued striving toward the "ideals" of the Sermon on the Mount, we are tempted to say, fulfill man's part of the contract. And when these are observed, conscience can rest at ease, leaving the further mysteries of religion to the pious and to those who want to make a specialty of doctrine or cult.

We must try to find a more apt equivalent. The Bible as a story about "covenants" does contain connotations of bargain and contract. God in the Bible makes promises, performs deeds of rescue, and then asks for obedience by way of response. But the context of such a *quid*

---

[3] I borrow this delightful phrase from a useful book on preaching by Canon S. P. T. Prideaux, *The Making of Sermons* (London: A. R. Mowbray & Co., 1947), p. 69. "Clement of Alexandria and Origen," so Canon Prideaux reports, though he does not give the reference, "quote an interesting saying of our Lord, that in the study of Scripture we are to be 'approved money-changers.'"

pro quo is not a law court or a counter over which merchandise is bought and sold. The context is a personal relationship. No personal relationship—no friendship or marriage, for example—is a mere legal transaction, or one that can be created by way of a *quid pro quo* even on the high level of moral conduct. Otherwise, there would be no meaning in Jesus' Parable of the Pharisee and the Publican, or in the Parable of the Prodigal Son, or in any act of divine salvation. All we would need is a set of legal statutes defining our side of the contract, which, if fulfilled, would guarantee God's grace. But love is never purchased in any such way.

The Bible as a Love Story

Is there any better synonym for the words "testament" and "covenant" than the word "relationship"? It is prosy, to be sure, and needs a poetic setting for full emotional effectiveness. A friend of mine, a rural missionary, translates the title page of the Bible as follows: "The Holy Book, containing the old and new love stories between God and man." The phrase "love story," to be sure, requires safeguards against mere "Hollywood" connotations. But how useful it is! The Bible, at least, employs the nuptial idea, or analogy, almost throughout—and with startling boldness. The revival of biblical theology in our era of Church history may, in fact, result in the recovery of the nuptial symbol as a major clue to the covenant relationship between God and His people. A contemporary scholar can say:

In modern theology it is common to speak almost exclusively of the Incarnation and of the Church in terms of St. Paul's image of the Body. . . . But this can never replace all the fullness of the Marriage. It cannot express the fundamental and original apartness of Man and the Word of God, nor the astounding love which impelled the Bridegroom to come down from heaven, to humble himself to the level of his creation. The Nuptial Idea includes the symbols of the Vine, the Body, the Building (City or Temple), the Household, and even the Sacrifice, the Ransom, and the Warrior Prince. It is the key to the treasure-house of the Church. The Sacrificial Idea has been retained; the Nuptial Idea has been forgotten. Today not one person in a thousand has ever seen an animal offered in sacrifice; but who has not assisted at a wedding? How strange it is that we miss this contact provided for us between ordinary life and the mysteries of God![4]

I shall not quote this author further, but I venture to underscore his insights. A connection can surely be traced between the title page of the Bible and the nuptial symbol. If relationship is the clue to the biblical revelation, we, the pastors and preachers of the Church, may possess a better understanding of the covenants of the Bible than our scholastic doctors. Relationships are our pastoral stock in trade. We are not strangers to wed-

[4] Claude Chavasse, *The Bride of Christ: An Enquiry into the Nuptial Element in Early Christianity* (London: Faber and Faber, 1939), pp. 16-18. Used by permission of the publisher.

dings or to marriage counselling or to life within families. Some one has called the Christian family "the little church," as, indeed, it is. These pastoral experiences
of ours can furnish us with incomparable analogies for
preaching the nature of the biblical covenants. The
nuptial analogy, neglected by much academic theology,
is truly a parable of the Kingdom, and the Bible utilizes
it almost throughout. We think first of Hosea's astounding insights into the problem of sin and the gospel of
redemption that he sets forth by means of the analogy
of a husband and his faithless wife. But the nuptial
analogy that Hosea employs can be traced both backward and forward. The central theme of the whole Old
Testament—Jahwe's relationship with a chosen people
—has nuptial connotations that break out in the writings of the prophets generally. Jeremiah has God, the
Lover, cry out: "I remember for thee the kindness of
thy youth, the love of thine espousals: how thou went-
est after me in the wilderness" (Jer. 2:2, ASV; cf. Jer.
3:8). Ezekiel echoes Hosea in the splendid imagery of
Chapter 16. The nameless prophet of the Exile pictures
the remarriage of Jahwe and Israel (Is. 61:10ff; 62:4ff.)
in lyrics which parallel the love poetry of the Song of
Songs or Psalm 45. And a whole chapter could be written on "The Marriage in the Gospels," and another on
the nuptial idea in St. Paul. The marriage parables of
Jesus, when interpreted with a messianic identification
of the Bridegroom, can unlock the secret of the whole
story of redemption—what has been called "The Drama

of the Victorious Bridegroom." [5] We come closer to the significance of the Church's eucharist in the story of its founding in the upper room and in the earliest Christian fellowships when we see it as the marriage feast of Christ and His Bride.[6]

The Authority of the Pulpit

I shall not trace further the nuptial idea in the Bible. We have traced it far enough to see that it can serve as incontrovertible proof of the fact that the clue to the Bible found on its title page is worthy of full exploitation. The Bible is not an encyclopaedia of knowledge. It is not a systematic textbook on religion, not even on the Christian religion. Philosophers and theologians can come to it with important questions, and yet find no clear answer. For the Bible is a love story. It concentrates upon the solution of one problem of human existence—the problem of relationships. It is a book— holy and sacred to those who live by its Good News— about *covenants*.

This fact, simple and yet profound, can bring great comfort to us, the preachers of the Church. We are overawed by speculative theology, but we need not be. Our academic theologians, as I have tried to argue ear-

[5] *Ibid.*, pp. 89ff.
[6] An echo of this primitive and biblical interpretation, lost, alas, in later liturgical development, is found in the earliest Anglican Prayer Book of 1549: "Wherefore let us kepe a joyfull and holy feast with the Lorde."

lier, have an important function in the life of the Church. They are the guardians of the faith against enemies. We need them to ensure that we, the proclaimers of the Gospel, be not "tossed to and fro and carried about with every wind of doctrine" (Eph. 4:14), but, instead, preach the true Good News. The Gospel, however, is the power of God unto salvation, not a speculative system of the schools.

The Church's pulpit, therefore, must stand guard over the saving Gospel. The Church's learned doctors need us, as we need them. Our protest against the tyranny of the intellect can save them from turning the Christian faith into an esoteric academic cult. Such a protest was once voiced by Luther's contemporary, Melanchthon, in a passage which is often cited and which still has contemporary relevance. Melanchthon had himself emerged from the prison house of late mediaeval scholasticism and rejoices in the revival of biblical theology in his revolutionary time. The passage, even though it is one-sided and may require corrective footnotes, can bring comfort to the preacher who is tempted to belittle his vocation:

If a man know nothing of the power of sin, of law, or of grace, I do not see how I can call him a Christian. It is there that Christ is truly known. The knowledge of Christ is to know his benefits, taste his salvation, and experience his grace; it is not, as the academic people say, to reflect on his natures and the modes of his incarnation. If you do not know the practical purpose for which he took flesh and went to his cross, what is the good of knowing his story? Is a doctor but a botanist? Is he content to know the forms and colours of his herbs? It is their virtue that counts. So with Christ. He is given as our remedy, or, in Bible phrase, our salvation. And we must know him in another way than the scholars. To know him to purpose is to know the demand of the conscience for holiness, the source of power to meet it, where to seek grace for our sin's failure, how to set up the sinking soul in the face of the world, the flesh, and the devil, how to console the conscience broken. Is that what any of the schools teach, metaphysical, critical, or literary? Paul in Romans, when he wants to condense Christian doctrine into a compendium, does he philosophize about the mysteries of the Trinity, or the method of incarnation, or an active and a passive creation? He does nothing of the kind. He speaks of law, sin and grace; of conscience, guilt and salvation. These are the topics on which a knowledge of Christ turns. You do not know Christ until you know these. How often Paul declares to his believers that he prays for them a rich knowledge of Christ. He foresaw that we should one day leave the saving themes and turn our minds to discussions cold and foreign to Christ. What we propose to do, therefore, is to sketch the inwardness of those passages that commend Christ to you, that settle the conscience, and establish the soul against Satan. Most people look in the Bible only for classic instruction about goodness and evil. But it is a philosophic more than a Christian quest.[7]

The clue to the Bible and its drama of salvation, I have suggested, can be found on its title page. This clue

[7] Preface to Melanchthon's *Loci* (1521). I have followed the translation in P. T. Forsyth's *The Person and Place of Jesus Christ* (Boston: The Pilgrim Press, 1909), pp. 220-22. Used by permission of the publisher.

is the word "covenant," which can be further translated "personal relationship." Can this key unlock the secrets of the theological vocabulary of the Christian faith?

The Doctrine of Sin

I venture to apply the clue, by way of example, to the concept of sin. A truly theological interpretation of the word "sin" is foreign to the modern mind. If the word is understood at all, it is as an immoral act, or a violation of an impersonal law. Sin, then, falls under what is called the juridic analogy, the analogy of the law court. God, in this analogy, frequently turns into a kind of Supreme Court Judge, and the Church into an ecclesiastical detective corps. Transactions between men and God turn into legal bargains—travesties of the covenant-religion of the Bible.

The Law, as argued in an earlier chapter, has an awesome part to play in the covenant story of the Bible. But this concept, and others flowing from it, must be personalized and interpreted by the primary biblical category of relationship. Seen thus, the problem of sins, or of *a* sin, gives place to a problem on a far deeper level of experience—namely, the problem of *Sin*. This concept still retains the word in the singular number, but capitalizes it to differentiate it from its derivatives. When thus given its full importance, the daring conclusion confronts us that *Sin,* in its full theological meaning, "does *not* mean an immoral act, that 'sin' should never be used in the plural, and that not our sins, but rather our *sin* is the great, all-pervading problem of life." [8] What then is Sin? I cannot do better than to let the author just quoted give his answer. He defines Sin—employing the clue of relationship—as "separation," and then continues:

Separation is an aspect of the experience of everyone. . . . To be in the state of sin is to be in the state of separation. And separation is three-fold: there is separation among individual lives, separation of a man from himself, and separation of all men from the Ground of Being. This three-fold separation constitutes the state of everything that exists; it is a universal fact; it is the fate of every life. And it is our human fate in a very special sense. For *we* as men know that we are separated. We not only suffer with all other creatures because of the self-destructive consequences of our separation, but also know *why* we suffer. We know that we are estranged from something to which we really belong, and with which we *should* be united. We know that the fate of separation is not merely a natural event like a flash of sudden lightning, but that it is an experience in which we actively participate, in which our whole personality is involved, and that, as fate, it is also *guilt*. Separation which is fate *and* guilt constitutes the meaning of the word 'sin.' It is *this* which is the state of our entire existence, from its very beginning to its very end. Such separation is prepared in the mother's womb, and before that time, in every preceding generation. It is manifest in the special actions of our conscious life. It reaches beyond

[8] Paul Tillich, *The Shaking of the Foundations* (New York: Charles Scribner's Sons, 1948), p. 154. Used by permission of the publisher.

our graves into all the succeeding generations. It is our existence itself. *Existence is separation!* Before sin is an act, it is a state.

Here, surely, is "theology for the preacher," theology that he can use to advantage, for it sheds light upon almost the whole panorama of the covenant vocabulary of the Bible and of classical theology. We all have had the experience of wishing to use, for example, a traditional phrase like original sin only to find that it means next to nothing to our contemporaries. In fact, it is met with rebellion. "What, burden an innocent child in the cradle with guilt for as yet uncommitted immoral acts?" they exclaim. "That violates even rudimentary human justice." And so it does, we must admit, if interpreted according to purely moralistic categories. The words "original sin," one ought to tell them, are not self-explanatory. The fact of existence that they attempt to describe is neither original, nor "a" sin. But use the phrase we must, and we can do so intelligibly only if we accompany the phrase with an explanation of the profound truth that it aims to convey. A child is born into a state of separation. Without grace—a word that invites interpretive translation also—a child dies. We are born self-centered beings. We are, as it were, little deities, rivals of the One God, rivals for the attention even of those who have brought us into the world.[9]

[9] The third chapter of Genesis pictures this "original" state of man after the Fall. The closing verses are particularly striking,

Robert Bridges, late poet laureate of England, pictures, in a noble poem, entitled "Pater Filio," this state of sin as we are able to see it even in a child still in his cradle. The first two stanzas read:

> Sense with keenest edge unused,
>   Yet unsteel'd by scathing fire;
> Lovely feet as yet unbruised
>   On the ways of dark desire;
> Sweetest hope that lookest smiling
> O'er the wilderness defiling!
>
> Why such beauty, to be blighted
>   By the swarm of foul destruction?
> Why such innocence delighted,
>   When sin stalks to thy seduction?
> All the litanies e'er chaunted
> Shall not keep thy faith undaunted.[10]

To rescue us from out of our state of separation and to bring us into a covenant relationship with God and man will require the whole drama of redemption. It will require as a first and climactic act being born again. We must walk through the waters of baptism—baptism symbolizing a dying to self and to the world of sin in which self rules, and a resurrection of the self in the new fellowship of repentance and forgiveness.

---

picturing God as actually jealous of a rival: "And the Lord God said, Behold the man is become as one of us, to know good and evil: and now, lest he put forth his hand, and take also of the tree of life, and eat, and live for ever; Therefore the Lord God sent him forth from the garden of Eden."

[10] *The Oxford Book of English Verse,* Number 838. Used by permission of the publisher.

Original Sin

The topic of baptism as, indeed, the drama of redemption as a whole, can here receive only brief allusion. My purpose, at the moment, limits itself to pointing out that the relationship concept in theology can rescue from the lumber room of faith's neglected treasures even so stubborn a concept as that of original sin. The doctrine of original sin has long been the scandal of theology for the modern mind. Yet, without the acceptance of this scandal, the biblical drama of salvation makes no sense. One can, with fair accuracy, date the rise of modernist undogmatic Christianity as paralleling that of the revolt against the doctrine of original sin. T. E. Hulme, a discerning critic of our modern age, has summarized this profound revolution in a passage that has been frequently cited. Hulme sharply divides two eras, the mediaeval and the modern, and defines the difference between them as fundamentally the difference between two conceptions of man. The first era believed in original sin; the second did not. Hulme observes:

It is necessary to realize the immense importance of this difference in belief, to realize that in reality almost everything springs from it. . . . There are certain doctrines which for a particular period seem not doctrines, but inevitable categories of the human mind. . . . For the Middle Ages these 'facts' were the belief in the subordination of man to certain absolute values, the radical imperfection of man, the doctrine of original sin.

The second period, our modern age, bases itself on a new conception of man as fundamentally good, as sufficient, as the measure of things. . . . Men's categories changed; the things they took for granted changed. Everything followed from that." [11]

This modern revolt against the doctrine of original sin becomes intelligible, and even excusable, only if sin is thought to be a mere problem of rationalistic ethics. The concept of man as "totally depraved"—a corollary that the doctrine of original sin seems to assert—is one that many find hard to accept. Indeed, the humanist will label it, without ado, "nonsense." And he is right if sin is nothing more than an immoral act. Goodness, defined as socially valuable conduct, is not a monopoly of reborn Christians! The Pharisee, in the famous parable of Jesus, was a good man, judged by the standards of legal morality. He was not guilty of sins in the sense of immoral acts. The publican carried that burden. When St. Paul describes Christian charity (a word which desperately needs "money-changing" in preaching) in the well-known chapter of his first Corinthian letter, he places over against it two unquestioned virtues—bestowing all one's goods to feed the poor, and giving one's body to be burned (I Cor. 13:3). And yet

[11] T. E. Hulme, *Speculations* (New York: Harcourt, Brace & Co., 1924), pp. 50ff. Used by permission of the publisher.

he says that these latter profit nothing. The highest of human virtues, in other words, can still not save a man from original sin.

A fateful confusion results in this whole area of religious concepts when the clue to their biblical meaning is lost—the clue of *relationship*. Sin is separation. Ignore the problem of separation, and a man can be good and virtuous, achieve all manner of victories over his lesser self, and yet be remanded to the "outer darkness" (Matt. 8:12) when he desires entrance into, what the New Testament calls, the kingdom of heaven. The debate whether Christianity has a pessimistic or optimistic view of man is clearly beside the point here. The real issue is self-centeredness of man as against his relationship with God. A self-centered man is a self-worshipper. (The Pharisee in the New Testament parable is described as even praying "with himself"!) The self that has become the center of his life may be a very good self, morally cultured and manicured. A god worthy of worship has to be on some kind of a throne, with a crown on his head, even if this god be a man's own ego. But such a god and his worshipper will lead a lonely life. "Be good and be lonely," reads a cynical epigram. It embodies a paradoxical truth, one which non-Christians frequently detect in Pharisaic piety. Loneliness is a foretaste of hell. The paradox that even a good man can be in hell seems startling, but it becomes meaningful as soon as we couple virtue with pride. The world has seen much proud virtue. And pride isolates a man from his neighbors and from God as does no other of the seven deadly sins.

The doctrine of original sin, rightly interpreted, far from embodying a low estimate of man, signifies the exact opposite. If the words "pessimism" or "optimism" can be applied to Christianity's view of human nature at all, the choice must be "optimism." For if sin means separation, the very experience and acknowledgment of sin, with its accompanying sense of guilt, testifies to the possibility of reunion. The story of the fall of man in Genesis, which lies back of the doctrine of original sin, contains good news for man, even though it delineates his present sad state. A fall—if guilt, as well as fate, is involved—clearly implies the possibility of rising again. A divorce presupposes a marriage. Separation, by definition, connotes a broken union. Hence there is truth in one of G. K. Chesterton's paradoxes: "The good news of the Gospel can be said to be the good news of original sin." [12] "No view of the human state," once said Bishop Westcott, "is so inexpressibly sad as that which leaves out the Fall. The existence of evil in its many forms, as self-will and suffering and vice and crime, cannot be gainsaid; and if evil belongs to the essence of man as created, then there can be no prospect of relief here or hereafter." [13] Or, to cite Chesterton once more: "If I wish to dissuade a man

[12] G. K. Chesterton, *Saint Francis of Assisi* (New York: George H. Doran Co., 1924), p. 39.
[13] B. F. Westcott, *Social Aspects of Christianity* (London: The Macmillan Co., 3rd ed., 1900), p. 12.

from drinking his tenth whiskey and soda, I slap him on the back and say, 'Be a man!' No one who wished to dissuade a crocodile from eating its tenth explorer would slap him on the back and say, 'Be a crocodile!' " [14]

The Doctrine of Grace

In any discussion of the topic of sin, we are very likely to encounter the word "grace." Can the theology of covenants or relationships throw light on this concept also? If my own experience is a true indication, few words in our Christian vocabulary are more puzzling to the layman.

Dictionary definitions are not of much help to people who want to understand the word, nor are the scholarly footnotes of Bible commentaries that trace the word back to its multiple meaning in the original Greek. The layman's difficulty arises from his forcing these definitions into his moralistic conception of Christianity. "Grace: Divine favor unmerited by man; a free gift of God for man's regeneration and sanctification," says Webster. Even if such definitions are verbally mastered, what have these to do with a religion of the Golden Rule, or the Sermon on the Mount, or the imitation of Jesus? The layman usually gets the impression from our sermons that we are urging him to secure *merited* favor with God. For why else should a man exert his

[14] Quoted by A. R. Vidler, in *Christian Belief* (New York: Charles Scribner's Sons, 1950), p. 32.

moral powers? But the very idea of "favor unmerited by man," if it means more than "our creation, preservation, and the blessings of this life," is something that upsets all honest moral accounting systems. Accordingly, when the layman hears us growing eloquent about grace, he labels it theology and hands it back to us experts. This is another of the pious red herrings of technical Church doctrine that so often spoil the perorations of our sermons.

A gigantic wall of misunderstanding faces us when we attempt to present the topic of grace from our pulpits. Nor will the piling of proof text upon proof text help us very much. A radical approach is needed here. Grace must be given its right context. It, like the word "sin," is not primarily a moralistic concept at all, though it will have, as do all theological concepts, a profound bearing upon moral conduct. Treat grace, however, as a fact of experience in the world of human relationships, and it steps forth from the dictionary into life.

If sin may be defined as separation, and rightly declared to be the basic problem of human existence, may not grace be the answer to this problem—namely, reunion?[15] It is certain, at least, that a whole cluster of words used in the Bible which belong to the category of grace have reunion as their theme. Memory quickly

[15] I again follow the lead here of Paul Tillich in his *The Shaking of the Foundations* (New York: Charles Scribner's Sons, 1948), p. 156.

parades them before us—*re*pentance, *re*generation, *re*-conciliation, *re*demption. The prefix *re*, common to the series, gives a clue to their meaning. Grace is the conquering something that restores a broken relationship. It is the answer to the alienation caused by sin. It is the miracle of true love, human and divine.

The clue, once boldly apprehended, can open floodgates for an inexhaustible stream of analogies on the human plane for the ultimate story of the "grace of our Lord Jesus Christ," for the doctrine of the atonement and its corollaries, the forgiveness of sins and salvation, as well as many more. We are at once in contact with life as it is being lived in palace or slum. Far from being an academic mystery of theology, grace is a necessity of existence, from the cradle to the grave, for every man, woman, and child in our parishes.

Illustrations of how the concept of grace as reunion can come alive in our sermons, as well as in the lives of our people, must surely crowd upon our imaginations. Every one of my readers could write his own anthology. I shall limit myself, accordingly, to a few pedagogic and homiletic suggestions.

Grace and Disgrace

The word "grace," as already hinted, has become for many a layman a relic in the vocabulary of piety that he finds enshrined in his Church's liturgy and hymns, since it has lost, for him, living meaning. This, however, is not true of its less shopworn opposite, the word "disgrace." Shakespeare's famous sonnet lines,

> When, in disgrace with fortune and men's eyes,
> I all alone beweep my outcast state,

describe experience as known to childhood, youth, and age. The loneliness of living in a state of disgrace—is there a mental torture worse than this? What is its source? Not necessarily a grievous moral lapse, though such a lapse may, of course, be one of its causes. Wearing a "wrong" dress at a party (surely, not necessarily a blameworthy moral lapse at all) may produce an excruciatingly painful feeling of disgrace. The somewhat puzzling wedding garment parable in the Gospels (Matthew 22:11-13) may receive meaning by recalling this simple fact of human experience. The clue to the meaning of disgrace, like the clue to its antonym "grace," is to place it in the context of relationship. We are in a state of disgrace when we suffer rejection by a group or a friend or members of our families or, on a deep level, by our own conscience. A relationship of acceptance has been broken, and we bear the burden of alienation. The standards by which such rejection has been motivated can, of course, vary, and these standards themselves must come under judgment. To be in disgrace with the fellowship of a group of gangsters differs profoundly from being in disgrace with the Fellowship of the Holy Spirit, yet the experience is, in some sense, similar. Our human relationships can still furnish analogies and parables for the kingdom of God, as they did when Jesus taught His disciples. "If ye then, *being evil,*" so Jesus daringly employs the device of analogy, "know how to give good gifts unto your children, *how much more* shall your Father which is in heaven give good things to them that ask him" (Matt. 7:11, ASV). Similarly, in preaching the Gospel, we can utilize, by way of illustration, the experience of men and women on their own level, even when this is evil. Disgrace, like its cure, is part of the raw stuff of social living. It is theology in terms of the language of relationship. Indeed, men and women who are supposedly illiterate in the academic language of theology may know more of what this language is really talking about than the sheltered professor of dogmatics or the sometimes equally sheltered preacher in bourgeois suburbia.

Grace, then, if we continue to wrestle with its meaning, is a healing of the hurt of disgrace. It is reunion. It brings an alien back into fellowship. It is a *crossing* (we can note the root syllable) of a gulf of separation. It is reconciliation, redemption, regeneration. Metaphor, parable, analogy—all crowd one upon the other in the Bible to illustrate the story of broken and restored relationships. And as the separation wrought by sin is threefold, reunion must be threefold. We cry out, in our state of disgrace and loneliness, for reunion with our fellow men, with our real selves, and, above all, with God; and these are interrelated. To understand this, we need merely to recall the double forgiveness of the Lord's Prayer, or St. John's plain words: "If a man say, I love God, and hateth his brother, he is a liar: for he that loveth not his brother whom he hath seen, how can he love God whom he hath not seen" (I John 4:20).

Doctrine in Parables

Have we as preachers the right to employ bold analogies of human relationships and call them theology? They can, admittedly, be dangerous. "For my thoughts are not your thoughts, neither are your ways my ways, saith the Lord" (Is. 55:8). Systematic theologians seem to fight shy of popularizing the doctrinal formularies of the Church by analogies taken from vulgar experience. They usually leave these risks to us. For them the rarefied atmosphere of scholastic rationalizing is safer; as indeed is that of moralizing for us. But this merely points to the need of a preached Gospel as a corrective to the theology of the schools. We have the example of the Master Teacher Himself. "All these things spake Jesus unto the multitudes in parables; and *without parable spake he not unto them*" (Matt. 13:34). And these parables are theology! The homiletic tradition of the Church has been tempted, even from the beginning, to transform the parables of Jesus into mere moral tales. The critical scholarship of our time is happily correcting this misunderstanding.[16]

Striking examples are the Parable of the Sower and the Parable of the Good Samaritan. The temptation to moralize the former, and thus to transform a parable of a sower into a parable of *soils,* was apparently irresistible even for the writers of the Gospels—possibly the earliest instance in Christian history of homiletic shying away from theology. For this parable, in Jesus' original intent, was, clearly, a parable on the doctrine of grace, not a *moral* exhortation. God's love is poured upon His world, regardless of the reception it receives. "He maketh his sun to rise on the evil and on the good, and sendeth rain on the just and on the unjust" (Matt. 5:45). God, the Sower, does not restrict the casting of His seed to falling on perfect soil only. He sows regardless—be the soil rocky or full of thorns or hard as the pavement of the wayside. St. Paul may well have used this parable to illustrate his Gospel text: "While we were yet sinners"—stony of heart and our lives choked with worldly idolatries—"Christ died for us" (Romans 5:8). The good news of unmerited love can, it is true, transform our hearts of stone into hearts of flesh only if it is received. A parable of soils can become

[16] See above, page 23f. Two modern books that can guard the preacher against the error of moralizing or allegorizing the parables are: B. T. D. Smith's *The Parables of the Synoptic Gospels* (Cambridge Univ. Press, 1937) and Charles W. F. Smith's *The Jesus of the Parables* (Philadelphia: The Westminster Press, 1948).

part of an enlarged analogy. But by itself it is not the primary good news of the story. Prepared soil? By all means. But this preparation is not "salvation by works." It is the broken and the contrite heart. And only God, coming with His unmerited love, can perform the task of heart-breaking. He is both Sower and Preparer of the soil. "Herein is love, not that we loved God, but that he loved us" (I John 4:10).

The Parable of the Good Samaritan furnishes another illustration of Jesus as Master Theologian. How grievously has this matchless story suffered homiletic mangling! Thousands of sermons have degraded this theological parable by treating it as a mere moral tale, useful, no doubt, to illustrate ethical idealism, but ignoring its awesome depth of meaning. "Go and do thou likewise" (Luke 10:37) is the text which we seize on as the story's climax. But *do* what? The point of the parable, clearly, is to be found in the contrast between the question asked by the lawyer and the question asked by Jesus at the end of the story. The lawyer is a legal moralist. Love of neighbor is Deuteronomic law. It must be obeyed if a man wishes to remain in the law-covenant with God. Hence the lawyer wants to see the law defined: "Who is my neighbor?" No law which a man can be expected to fulfill can be infinite, since then there could be no passing grade. If—as St. Paul will later draw the conclusion from Jesus' teachings—all men "have sinned and fall short of the glory of God" (Romans 3:23, RSV), it looks as if legal moralism is bankrupt and no salvation by works possible. The lawyer resembles Peter in the scene in which the disciple asks Jesus to define the limits of the law of forgiveness: "How oft shall my brother sin against me, and I forgive him? until seven times?" The reply of Jesus to Peter, like His reply to the lawyer, must have seemed shocking: "I say not unto thee, until seven times; but until seventy times seven" (Matt. 18:22). In other words, the obligation is infinite.

The problem of law-religion, then, sets the scene for the Parable of the Good Samaritan. At the close of the story Jesus confronts the lawyer with the question: "Which now of these three, thinkest thou, *was neighbour* unto him that fell among the thieves?" The Samaritan had not asked the question: "Who is my neighbour?" He simply *was* a neighborly person, with a love that went out to the needy regardless of their social status or even their moral worth. It has often been noted that the victim in the story remains anonymous and is not described or characterized. The good Samaritan foreshadows the new creature in Christ of Christian faith— one transformed within and reborn into citizenship in the kingdom of God where love fulfills the law. His love of neighbor resembles God's love, which also asks no questions as to the status or worth of men *before* it makes grace available to sinners. St. Paul could have taken the Samaritan as symbol of the Christian life: "Therefore be ye imitators of God, as beloved children. And walk in love, even as Christ loved us" (Eph. 5:1,2,

RSV). But such imitation of God is not achieved by un-
transformed human nature. It requires regeneration, a
dying to self, and a resurrection. The lawyer in the
story, like Peter listening to the precept of infinite forgiveness, must have stood crushed before our Lord's
demand. As obedience to an infinite demand, performance is, indeed, impossible. Jesus did not see the kingdom realized in His lifetime even among His own disciples. He, alone on the Cross, became the exemplar of
the good Samaritan. Flowing from the Cross, however,
this Christ-life of a love which "seeketh not its own"
did appear in later history, incompletely realized, it is
true, yet visible to men. Peter, the legalist, aghast before
the demand for infinite forgiveness, becomes Peter the
apostle and witness and martyr, transformed within.
We may be certain that as a new man "in Christ," he
no longer asked: "How oft shall I forgive?" And in the
Church of apostolic founding, the good Samaritan has,
by the power of the Christ-life within the fellowship,
been actualized uncounted times.

The above paragraphs did not aim to bring onto the
scene an exhaustive analysis of the parables of Jesus.
The two examples cited may suffice, however, as proof
of the fact that parables can be profound theology. The
linking together of St. Paul and Jesus is no accident. To
suppose that we can find in the teachings of Jesus a
simple moralistic and undogmatic gospel of ethical
idealism is an illusion. The parables of the Gospels

lead directly into the dogmatic Christianity of the Epistles. The best commentary on the parables may well be St. Paul's Epistle to the Romans!

Theology by Analogy

To return, then, to the modern preacher. We of the twentieth century cannot employ parables in quite the way in which they were current in the rabbinic schools of Jesus' time. The masterpieces of the Gospels remain unique. But Jesus as Master Teacher can be our model still. Parables come under the more generalized category of analogies. These, in forms which fit our age, are not denied us. No interpreter of the Christian faith will be more gratefully welcomed by the layman of today than one of whom it can be said, "Without a parable spake he not unto them." But a warning is needed. As the parables of Jesus are theological parables—parables of the kingdom of God, and not merely good advice or moral tales—so the art of analogy should be directed in our day to a disclosure, in terms of everyday living, of the height and depth of the Gospel of salvation.

Nor is this an impossible task. Our theme, before it suffered interruption by way of a defense of the art of analogy, was sin and grace. These are not academic topics. A child of two years experiences the tragedy of disgrace and the miracle of reconciliation as vividly as any adult. Yet bring the child into a Sunday school and assault it with the word-symbols of technical theology, or even of an uninterpreted Bible, and a gulf may be created between experience and symbol which may well remain a hindrance through life. Translation is a literally desperate need. The language of words and the language of relationship must become reunited.

I venture to present an experiment in teaching by parable out of my own pedagogic workroom. I have, on occasion, called it "The Parable of the Flower Shop."

Few terms found in the Bible or in theological textbooks would appear further removed from daily life than the word "propitiation" (Rom. 3:25; I John 2:2; 4:10). It appears at first, even when looked up in a dictionary, to be a fossil-word, belonging to the ancient world of Hebrew religion, but now long outgrown even in Judaism. Historians may find the story of propitiatory sacrifice a fascinating anthropological hobby, but what can propitiatory sacrifice mean to us today? The word "propitiation" appears, to be sure, in one of the Comfortable Words of the Book of Common Prayer: "If any man sin, we have an Advocate with the Father, Jesus Christ the righteous; and he is the Propitiation for our sins" (I John 2:1,2). Yet one may fairly doubt whether one layman in a thousand, on hearing these words, relates this word "propitiation" to his own experience. Here, surely, is a traditional theological word that is unconnected with contemporary life.

But apply here the art of analogy and the word "propitiation" sheds its hoary garments and steps forth as vivid universal fact. A schoolboy in disgrace with his teacher places a "polished" apple on the teacher's awesome desk. Propitiatory sacrifice! A husband is on his way home, late for dinner, with a doubtful excuse. He stops at a flower shop and buys a dozen roses for his offended wife. Propitiatory sacrifice! Florists might be amazed to learn that they are dependent for a fair portion of their income upon a ritual of propitiation that traces back to the dawn of time.

Propitiatory sacrifice, as a matter of fact, is related to a whole class of sacrificial acts which are today as clearly sacrifices as when bullocks and goats were slaughtered on altars of stone. No relationship between persons is ever without sacrificial symbols—gifts brought to metaphorical shrines to win acceptance or to bridge a gulf of broken trust. A young man rings the door bell of his beloved with a box of candy in his hand. His is a wooing sacrifice, one given in order to establish a relationship of love. Nor do we limit our sacrificial rites to our mutual relationships on the human plane. We still sacrifice to the gods—all too frequently to pagan deities and idols. Many a Sunday school class has been horrified by the story of Abraham's sacrifice of his son Isaac. The teacher explains away the literal details as belonging to an age of primitive religion, and the story is then neatly moralized. Yet the sacrifice of children may be going on in the very community in which the children have their homes. The children in the Sunday school may themselves be sacrificial victims—a son that is sacrificed to the idol of a father's ambition, or a

daughter to a mother's social career. The gods of suburbia, idols of the religion of "keeping up with Joneses,"
demand a veritable holocaust of victims.

Propitiatory sacrifice—to return to this specific form
of sacrificial acts—becomes fully meaningful when a
broken relationship is involved. The husband late for
dinner with a bad conscience may present only a mild
problem of reunion. The issue becomes acute when the
break in relationship approaches a final separation. An
unbridged chasm looms. The divorce statistics of the
land confront "the ministry of reconciliation" (II Cor.
5:18) of the Church with an almost unbearable demand for help. When the story is one of the final breaking of bonds, propitiatory sacrifice is soon found to be
ineffective. The way of bargain from guilt to forgiveness
is blocked. Grace must take the place of bargain. Reconciliation requires a gift—as, indeed, the very word
"forgiveness" indicates. The greater the gulf in a broken
relationship, the more costly will be the gift. How can
right cross over to the side of wrong? Or holiness to
the side of sin? Even on the human plane it is an action
that costs and pays a price. Think for a moment of a
husband breaking a wife's heart through an act of
treachery to his marriage vow. He may suffer remorse
and try propitiatory sacrifices—a gift of flowers being
climaxed with more costly symbols of contrition. Will
these gifts bridge the gulf between them? They may,
indeed, be tokens of need and a cry for reconciliation.
But that is all. The reconciling act must come from the

wife, as sheer gift, sheer grace. Many a guilty husband has had to come to a wronged marriage partner with a paraphrase of the words of the familiar hymn:

> In my hands no price I bring;
> Simply to thy cross I cling.

The sequel to a drama of repentance and forgiveness may, however, if it has ended in the joy of reconciliation, be a new kind of sacrifice—the sacrifice of gratitude. The husband, if he should again seek out the flower shop for a symbol of his need, may now buy dozens of roses and heap them upon his wife's lap. Propitiatory sacrifice has been, by a miracle of grace, transformed into a sacrifice of praise and thanksgiving.

The analogy, or parable, is, of course, but a frail human insight into the drama of the redeeming Cross of Christ.[17] When we try to envisage what it cost God to enact His crossing of the gulf from His holiness to our fallen state, imagination falters. But this *is* the Gospel story. The Son of God, Deity in the flesh, dwells among us and does not turn His face away. He dines with publicans and sinners. He accepts a criminal's

---

[17] The analogy, in fact, requires at least one important corrective footnote. Forgiveness on the human plane alone, outside the covenant of God's prevenient grace, is either impossible, or threatened by perversion into pride. It may be nothing more than an illustration of the Aristotelian virtue of magnanimity, and may lead to a lording it over the sinner, by burdening him with an obligation which he can never repay. Only a sinner forgiven can really forgive. Yet the fact that our human analogies of the Kingdom (we being "evil") are never without danger of distortion should not prevent our employing them in faith. Even Jesus ran the risk of being misunderstood.

death at our hands—and yet forgives. All of our human analogies are but seeing through a glass darkly as we approach this ultimate mystery of the drama of redemption. Yet even when we see it only falteringly, it has the power to usher us into the forecourts of heaven. "If any man sin, we have an Advocate with the Father, Jesus Christ the righteous; and he is the Propitiation for our sins."

CHAPTER IV

Faith and "The Faith"

A reader of the foregoing chapters may have noticed that the word "theology" has been the victim of ambiguity—a fact symbolized by its appearing, on occasion, within quotation marks. There are, in Christian tradition and experience, so it appears, two "theologies." One of these is the proper object of study of the Church's guardians of doctrine, those teachers set apart as an academic caste. The other is the birthright of every member of the Church, even one who cannot read or write. We are here dealing, clearly, with a paradox that must concern the preacher of the Gospel. Can it be further clarified?

Every Man Lives by Faith

One method of clarification is to examine the related paradox that confronts us when dealing with the concept "faith." Indeed, faith is a word constantly on the preacher's lips. What is his vocation, as minister of the

Word, except that of presenting the faith of the Church to his people and persuading them to accept it? Yet a confusion has already attached itself to the concept "faith" when we look at its use in the preceding sentence. The article "the" has been prefixed to it. Faith, without the article, is a verb-noun denoting an action that involves the will. Helpful synonyms are words like trust or commitment or allegiance. The whole person, the mysterious being who can say "I," is involved in an act of faith. Nor is faith limited to Christians or to those who "have religion" (as the saying goes). Every man lives by faith—even the atheist and the suicide. It is conspicuous in idolatry, even when the idol is not consciously acknowledged or named.

When the article *the* is prefixed to the word "faith," however, we enter a different world. Expand the phrase to "the Church's faith" or "the Christian faith," and we encounter academic theology, with its systems of dogma and doctrine, its creeds and confessions. The foundation upon which the Christian faith has been constructed in the course of the Church's history is the Bible—the Bible accepted as the inspired Word of God. *The* Christian faith, accordingly, could be verbalized and taught, and faith, as an act of commitment, came to be understood as the acceptance of such a formulation as true. A confession—in the technical sense of a profession of faith—usually consisted of a compendium of propositional "truths," each one buttressed by a biblical text as proof. We do our fathers in the faith a wrong, to be sure, when we accuse them of limiting the Christian life only to an academic discipline or mere verbal commitment. Commandments of the Lord demanding obedience, exhortation to moral striving, confession of sin, and belief in the Good News of forgiveness were an essential part of biblical revelation and, as such, evoked response. But, for them, subscription to a verbalized formula came first.

Does envy of the lot of the preacher as this is reflected in the sermon literature of former centuries assault us on occasion? Theirs was plain sailing. "They had," so A. C. Craig, in his recent Warwick Lectures, puts it, "to preach the fundamentals of the faith as these were revealed in Scripture and had been reduced to dogmatic form in the confessional documents of the Church. The whole structure was marvellously massive and coherent, like a Norman castle. Like a Norman castle, too, it was unembellished and somewhat grim of aspect." [1]

But for us of the twentieth century, who are inheritors of a century and more of historical criticism of the Bible, this tidy, though majestic, preaching of dogma and doctrine has become impossible. As an earlier chapter indicated, a revolution has occurred in our very conception of revelation. The deposit of fact upon which is built *the* Christian faith (whatever that now may

[1] A. C. Craig, *Preaching in a Scientific Age* (London: Student Christian Movement Press, 1954), p. 19.

mean) is seen to be a story, a drama, what a Collect of the Book of Common Prayer terms "the mighty acts of God." Dorothy Sayers has reminded us, in her vivid pamphlet pleading for a dogmatic Christianity, that "the dogma *is* the drama." [2] This story of God's acting in history can be distilled, to be sure, into propositional form, as it has been in various systems of divinity in the Church's history, yet the Bible itself lends us only moderate encouragement in this. Theology in the Bible is *recital* theology[3]—the recital of God's actions in the history of the world and of His people. Typical of this in the Old Testament is Psalm 78: "I will open my mouth in a parable; I will declare hard sentences of old, . . . to show the honor of the Lord, his mighty and wonderful works that he hath done. He made a covenant with Jacob, and gave Israel a law, which he commanded our forefathers to teach their children" (Psalm 78:2, 4-5). Typical in the New Testament are the sermons of Peter and of Paul: "We declare unto you glad tidings, how that the promise which was made unto the fathers, God hath fulfilled the same unto us their children, in that he hath raised up Jesus" (Acts 13:32,33). Remove the Red Sea rescue and the Resurrection from the Bible and its theology collapses.

[2] Dorothy Sayers, *The Greatest Drama Ever Staged* (London: Hodder and Stoughton, 1938), p. 6.

[3] The phrase summarizes the main theme of G. Ernest Wright's monograph, in the field of biblical theology, *God Who Acts* (Chicago: Henry Regnery Co., 1952).

Faith Without Dogma

But the rediscovery of the verb-theology of the Bible is still something of a novelty in many schools, and even more in the pulpit. It will take us all some time to embody in our preaching its profound significance.

In the meantime, in the interval between the breakdown of biblical literalism and the contemporary emergence of biblical theology, what happened to the concept of faith—faith, that is, as trust and commitment and as an active practice of religion resulting from sermon or classroom presentation? Clearly, a sweeping emancipation from such a concept was the first effect. Most ministers who trace their younger years back to the early decades of our century can testify to the exhilaration of freedom from dogma and creed and tyrannizing orthodoxy that marked that era. "A practical Christianity at last!" so it was said. Woe to the hypocrites in our churches who were experts in orthodoxy and who examined candidates for ministerial appointments on minutiae of confessional belief and yet listened unmoved to the Sermon on the Mount or seemed never to have heard of love as the fulfillment of the law. Faith, to be sure, was once more a verb-noun. But faith or trust in what? The question was not always asked: were the objects of allegiance and devotion not obvious enough —for those, at least, who had the piety of orthodoxy still in their blood? The acids of biblical criticism had not touched the moral idealism of our Christian past, nor the human appeal of Jesus. The social gospel stood ready to absorb any loyalties left over from individualist commitments to high ends. But it was a faith without dogma, a faith in Christian man, with God only vaguely in the background and scarcely needed. Christianity had reverted to a kind of sentimental Judaism—a Judaism of ideals in place of divine commandments, a moralistic humanism in which a human hero called Jesus had replaced the awesome Jahwe of Sinai and of the prophets.

But, as earlier chapters have argued, this emancipated Christianity of faith without dogma in its turn broke down. We need not mourn the passing of the era of biblicist orthodoxy. The Church of the future may some day enshrine in its register of heroes those who, in the course of the dethronement of this theology, dared to risk their soul's salvation in loyalty to scientific and historical truth, even though some became actual casualties and suffered loss of faith. The term *liberalism* that we attach to this recent period of Church history and that has gathered about itself an aura of heresy may again become a symbol of victory. Yet we do, as ministers of the Word, stand at the threshold of a new age. Once more we ask how we can find ourselves at home in it.

We are confronted by an apparently impossible paradox. The era of liberalism had restored to us the concept of faith as an action involving the will and one not to be confused with subscription to a system of divinity or to merely verbalized doctrines. Yet faith without

dogma—faith without theology—has proved equally
wanting. We are, in fact, being asked to return to a
theological gospel. Can the paradox find further solution? An attempted solution has found partial expression in previous chapters. Here it remains, even at the
risk of some repetition, to make this more explicit and
to place it in the larger context of the Church's ongoing
life.

Dogma—as heirs of the revolt against confessional
theology, we are frightened by the word. But if we take
seriously the insight of contemporary biblical theology
—namely, that the dogma central to the Christianity of
the New Testament is verb-dogma, and is, like faith
itself, an action with a plot, suspicion even of the word
may be transformed into joyous acceptance. One could
wish for a less austere word to define the heart of
Christianity's message. The connotations of the word
"dogma" seem to smother the understanding of faith
as a personal relationship. Yet we cannot do without
it. It is the symbol of that something on which faith,
understood as trust, if it is to be the faith-act of the
Christian, depends. Acceptance of some propositional
formulation as buttress to faith as trust will be inevitable, though such acceptance must at once be transformed into its correlative in act and deed and personal
commitment. The New Testament is not a textbook in
systematic divinity, let us grant. But the central dogma
of Christian faith stands there just as surely as if carved
in granite. Three words define it: "Jesus is Lord."

The dogma enshrined in the New Testament, we say, is drama, and the drama is the dogma. This drama, however, has, as chief actor, God, not man. All the warfare against heresy in the early centuries of the Church's life—sheer abracadabra to many modern Christians—centered on preserving the recognition of Jesus as both fully God and fully man. This looks as if a school of technical theologians had tried to turn the simple story of Jesus into a philosophical system that only the Church's future seminary professors could understand. Yet the issue is one by which the humblest believer's faith stands or falls. If Jesus was merely a man, even the best in all history, His heroic life and death might be biographically inspiring, but it could not be a revelation of God's love. It would not be Good News, since the world has seen thousands of good men suffer. Undeserved tragedy and pain is precisely the basis for the indictment *against* trust in a God of love that the sceptics of all ages have hurled at believers. The heresy of Arius and his followers, which precipitated the formulation of the Nicene Creed, consisted in a refusal to go further in recognizing Jesus as fully God than to call Him a being *like* God. But this would still have left the indictment against belief in a God who "cared" unanswered. God would have merely assigned some one other than Himself to die on a cross for love of men. The authentic good news of the Gospel has been summarized in two words: "God cares." The ultimate proof in action of this caring is, according to Christian faith,

Christ's death upon the Cross. This event in history is Good News only if the dogma of the Incarnation—the doctrine that Jesus is fully God, as well as fully man—remains starkly intact.

The Verb-Theology of the Bible

But recognition of a person as actor in a story is itself an action and not merely intellectual assent to a propositional truth. Thousands have read the gospels of the New Testament and have seen in them nothing more than the life story of a Jewish rabbi, whose teachings belong to the cultural wisdom literature of mankind. Recognizing God incarnate in the human Jesus demands a leap of faith—particularly since such recognition involves penetrating a disguise or an incognito. Yet a child can perform this act of recognition as well as a professor of dogmatics. Such an act of recognition differs in kind from mere intellectual assent to an argued proposition, though, the recognition once made, it can, of course, be accorded propositional formulation: "I believe *that* the Jesus of the Gospel story is the eternal Son of God." It is surely significant that the historic creeds of the Church employ the language of personal trust: "I believe *in* Jesus Christ our Lord." The creeds are acts of allegiance. Basic Christian dogma remains action-faith. It involves personal encounter, knowing, seeing, obeying, prayer.[4]

⁴ Anglicans are fond of quoting, on this issue of the meaning of the historic creeds, one of Anglicanism's wisest theologians of

The above excursus on the dogma of the Incarnation is but one illustration of the paradoxical relationship between "faith" and "the faith." It may, indeed, have been presented prematurely, since, central to Christianity though it be, it is only part of a larger whole. One may doubt whether any convert to Christianity ever grasped its meaning on encountering it when abstracted from that whole—a fact which the preacher of the Gospel should realize.

Let us look at the paradox, then, from another angle of vision. We are to proclaim a gospel leading to faith as action. But faith in what? In action as such, motivated by a moral idealism vaguely inherited from the Christian tradition? That was Liberalism's error. Eventually it proves to be faith in man, in ourselves as our own saviours. It has no answer to the problem of death, or that of sin. It must be confronted with faith in God —and not faith in any god either, but faith in the God of biblical revelation.

---

the last century, Frederick Denison Maurice. A typical passage, envisaging a man who might meet the Creed in print or by ear for the first time, reads: "He will find, I think, that it differs from all digests of doctrines, whether religious or philosophical, which he has ever seen. A man is speaking in it. The form of it is, I believe. That which is believed in is not a certain scheme of divinity, but a name—a Father, who has made the heaven and the earth: His Son, our Lord, who has been conceived, born, and died . . . a Holy Spirit, who has established a holy universal Church. . . . The Creed is evidently an act of allegiance. . . . The Creed has served as a protection to the humbler members of the Church against the inclination which the Church doctors of different ages have manifested to rob them of their inheritance and to appropriate it to themselves." (*The Kingdom of Christ* (Everyman Edition), II, pp. 4 and 15.)

The Dogma of the Incarnation

Here, clearly, is "theology for the preacher." The concept of faith itself as the trust-act by which every man lives can be explored, as can the idolatries of our time. Whole areas of Old Testament prophecy (e.g., Isaiah 40-66, climactical for idol-smashing texts) can come to life. I present this fascinating theme for preaching by title. Every minister of the Word can readily fill out its implications. Over against faith in idols, the preacher will then present faith in the God of Christians. This God is known to us, the people of God, in the story of the Bible. And the story can be told, from Creation to coming Last Judgment. Here they are, the mighty acts of God, revelation in deed of Who He is. Our preached theology becomes what it so largely was for the "preachers" of the Bible itself—recital theology. Such proclamation has, as its objective, the leading of the listener to his own personal surrender. Hence it must always be something more than abstracted doctrine. "It is," Emil Brunner suggests, "faith-awakening, faith-furthering, faith-wooing address." [5]

Can such a return of the sermon to proclamation—to the recital theology of the Bible itself—save us from some of the futilities of modern preaching? How tempting it has been to take an isolated Bible text, some

[5] Emil Brunner, *The Divine-Human Encounter* (Philadelphia: The Westminster Press, 1943), p. 174.

snippet of a story in Judges, or the Books of the Kings, or in the life of Jesus, and to by-pass its meaning as revelation of God, employing it, instead, as a springboard for moral exhortation, for berating the evils of the day or for purposes of soporific "spiritual" uplift. As if knowledge of good and evil or flattery of man's innate goodness were Good News! We can profit from the insight of Luther, writ large in the Bible as well, when he names unbelief as our basic human problem. Faith-surrender to God must come first, or else all of our mani-curing of morals may merely turn a few more publicans into proud and obnoxious Pharisees. The objective of our preaching must be a wooing of the stubborn wills of men and women to a dying to self, to repentance, and to rebirth as sons of God.

But to make the recital theology of the Bible the content of our proclamation, its objective a wooing to faith-surrender to the *right* God—this is not an easy task. One reason why many of us have been tempted into homiletic by-paths is precisely its awesome diffi-culty. To encounter the God of the Bible in face to face dialogue—my "I" with His "Thou"—do we ourselves not shrink from such a meeting? "Tell me the old, old story of Jesus and His love," so we sing the familiar gospel hymn. Quite so, provided that the story of His love remains true to the definitive dogma of the In-carnation. But even a meeting face to face with the re-membered Jesus of past history (granted the possibility) would not, if we read the Gospel record with open eyes, be exactly an amiable encounter. Some one has suggested that we can get a little insight into the effect of Jesus upon His contemporaries if we imagine the voice speaking in our conscience taking on human form and confronting us as a person. For He was God incarnate —the Jahwe of Mount Sinai, of Amos and Jeremiah. Has our modernist preaching of Jesus ever taken this fact into account with sufficient seriousness? The dogma of the Incarnation—Jesus is Lord—is still, it appears, scandal and stumbling block for us as it was for the Jew and the Greek of the first century. Yet the whole meaning of the biblical drama of salvation hinges upon this scandal. When the scandal is taken seriously, confrontation with the Jesus of the New Testament becomes awesome encounter, indeed. One of the closing chapters of the Old Testament, looking forward to the coming of the Messiah, described it rightly:

The Lord, whom ye seek, shall suddenly come to his temple, even the messenger of the covenant whom ye delight in. But who may abide the day of his coming? and who shall stand when he appeareth? for he is like a refiner's fire.—Malachi 3:1,2

Rediscovering the Old Testament

One of the most grievous pitfalls into which much modernist preaching has fallen is that of ignoring the Old Testament background of the life of Christ. It takes only a fresh look at the New Testament as a whole to realize that even the disciples were not "Christians" until after the Resurrection and Pentecost. Before those climactic events they were Jews. They were still under the tutelage of the Law—the Schoolmaster "until Christ came" (Gal. 3:24, rsv). Whenever we neglect the revelation of God as given us in the Old Testament, we do hurt to the Gospel of the New Testament as well. We are in danger of preaching what Dietrich Bonhoeffer calls "cheap grace." [6] Indeed, if we take courage and present the wrath of God as honestly as we present His love, we may find that our listeners will hail both as good news. Judgment and grace are sides of the same coin. It is dawning slowly upon a godless world that its tragedy consists precisely in the fact that it has no Judge. An honest observer of those who, in our post-Christian era, have lost their anchorage in the Christian faith epitomizes the agnostic's dilemma and his anxiety in a meaningless universe in four vivid words: "No modern can sin." [7] For sin implies a Judge, and judgment implies a relationship of caring—a covenant of grace. Has our human lot, already redeemed from meaninglessness under a covenant of judgment (and even of wrath) ever received more moving description than in the opening verses of the fourteenth chapter of the Book of Job?

[6] Dietrich Bonhoeffer, *The Cost of Discipleship* (New York: the Macmillan Co., 1949), pp. 37-49, a chapter on "Costly Grace."

[7] Joseph Wood Krutch, *The Modern Temper* (Harcourt, Brace & Co., 1929), p. 134.

Man that is born of a woman is of few days and full of trouble. He cometh forth like a flower and is cut down: he fleeth also as a shadow, and continueth not. And dost thou open thine eyes upon such an one, and bringest me into judgment with thee?

The story of the Gospels, read with the dogma of the Incarnation as a clue, is a fulfillment of Job's cry for a God who cares enough to search us out even when, like Adam, we hide amongst the trees of the garden. "The Word was made flesh and dwelt among us" (John 1:14). He came as holiness incarnate. He tracked sin to its lair in the innermost chambers of man's heart. The marvel is that even when "his own received him not," He did not turn His face away. He did not pray the Father for a new flood to destroy rebellious man as in the days of Noah. He "endured the cross, despising the shame" (Hebrews 12:2).

It may, to be sure, look like vandalism applied to the Bible to suggest (for pedagogic and homiletic purposes only, of course) that the division between the two testaments should come at the break between the Gospels and the Acts of the Apostles. Yet the device would clarify much misunderstanding. The New Testament, as literally the new *covenant,* did not become a revealed mystery until after the Cross and the Resurrection. The matchless story of the life of Jesus, until it could be climaxed in the Cross, is still, if we read the record as it was experienced by the disciples, the closing scene of the covenant of Sinai. Jesus Himself was conscious of

His twofold mission—that of fulfillment of the Law (what has been called Christ's "strange work") and that of ushering in the covenant of reconciliation. But the latter awaited His death.[8] "I have a baptism to be baptized with; and how am I straitened till it be accomplished. Suppose ye that I am come to give peace on earth? I tell you, Nay, but rather division" (Luke 12:50,51).

Rediscovering the New Testament

It is only with the Resurrection and Pentecost that the apostolic era opens. A strange new world it was for the disciple group, and may still be for us. Even the beloved name of Master had to be relegated to the chamber of memory. For now He, who had been Companion, Teacher, Friend, was revealed as Son of God. A future meeting was shortly expected, but it would be unlike the remembered meetings on a lake shore. He would come again on the clouds of heaven, as Judge of the living and the dead. "We have known Christ after the flesh," so St. Paul summarizes the contrast between the days of Jesus as Master and the new era of Jesus as ascended Lord, "yet now henceforth know we him no more" (II Cor. 5:16). The march in time of the mighty acts of divine revelation could not be reversed. The Resurrection had unveiled Jesus as the

[8] See A. R. Vidler's *Christ's Strange Work* (London: Longmans, Green & Co., 1944).

Christ. The Ascension had removed Him from even post-Resurrection companioning.

We are, so runs our familiar charter for the ministry of the Word, to "preach Christ." But if the Ascension has removed Him from our earthly scene, how is a personal meeting possible? Sentimental memory, clearly, is no substitute. The apostolic era, at least, did not indulge in sentimental longing for the vanished Master-disciple relationship. Are we then, if apostolic faith is to be recovered as our norm, compelled to turn the Gospel from confrontation with the Person of Christ into acceptance of doctrines *about* Christ? Are we back to the dilemma of deciding between a personal faith rooted in event and an impersonal acceptance of propositional truths? Is there after all no release from the tyranny of school theology? Can the New Testament itself yield no solution to the problem?

Any reader, familiar with the New Testament, will, of course, be able to remind us that, fortunately for us who cannot reverse time and who cannot re-create, except in nostalgic memory, the days of the Galilean disciple group, the drama of revelation did not end with the Crucifixion. But before these climactic events are brought fully upon the scene, a word may well be said about the dogma of the Incarnation which our argument has assumed to be the rock upon which the Christian faith is built. This, too, like the life of Jesus abstracted from the later acts of the drama, needs supplementation. "Jesus is Lord and God" remains as the

basic confession of Christian faith. It names and identi-
fies the Actor in the drama, but it is not yet the drama
itself. Nor is it, by itself, as yet the heart of the good
news of the Gospel.

Emil Brunner is worth listening to on this issue, crucial for our preaching the authentic good news of the
New Testament:

The Incarnation as such is not the pivotal point of the
Biblical revelation, but rather the *work* of the Redeemer.
Jesus Christ did not come merely to come, but He came to
redeem. To be sure, only the Incarnate Lord—very God,
very man—can be the Redeemer. But the Bible guides us
to ponder less the secret of the Person of Christ than the
mystery of His work. . . . Not the substantive, but the
verb is the chief word in Biblical language.[9]

The *work* of Christ. Here at last, so it seems, we
enter the holy of holies of the New Testament Gospel.
This we must preach, or prove apostate to Christian
faith. Are not our memories, if still fed by the Church's
liturgies and hymns, crowded with awesome words
which declare this good news? The title page phrase
"New Testament" already announces it—a new relationship between sinner and holy God, wrought out in
the life work of the Son of God and left us as a legacy
on His departure. "God was in Christ reconciling the
world unto himself" (II Cor. 5:19)—is there, in a
phrase, a more breath-taking summary of the apostolic

[9] Emil Brunner, *The Divine-Human Encounter* (Philadelphia:
The Westminster Press, 1943), p. 142. Used by permission of
the publisher.

proclamation which conquered the ancient world? *The* Gospel is this resultant, this *work* of the Redeemer. All honors paid to Him as Person, all loyalty which we can muster as followers or disciples, are sentimental futilities unless they are the fruit of our having entered into a relationship with the Father through His reconciling act. Otherwise our good works can be for us damnation, repetitions of the age-old attempt to bridge the chasm between sinner and holy deity by our own prideful efforts.

The Doctrine of Justification

Has there ever been a Christian believer that has truly experienced the wonder of the Gospel who has not known in his heart that the gulf between his guilty conscience and the God of holiness could have been bridged only by Him and not by the sinner? The doctrine of justification by faith has caused much anguish in the course of Christian history. But if the concept of justification by faith—not the most easily understood phrase in the vocabulary of religion, one must admit— is given meaning by way of analogies of personal relationship, is it less than a summary of the Good News of Christ's reconciling Cross? Legalistic or juridic analogies make nonsense of it. Abstracted from the drama of the Bible as a whole, the doctrine of justification by faith can lead, as history proves, to grave misunderstandings. It might be well for us, as preachers, to employ as basic Scriptural text the enlarged version in the Epistle to the Ephesians (2:8-10): "By grace are ye saved through faith . . . unto good works"—grace from God's side in the forgiveness extended to the sinner; faith, on man's side, in the trust-surrender of repentance; good works the fruit of the restored relationship.

This central doctrine of the New Testament, more than, perhaps, any other in the deposit of Christian teaching, has been the victim of the confusion between faith and *the* faith. "Justification by *the* faith," by the signing on the dotted line of a theological proposition—this, surely, is a travesty of the Gospel. Or, in turn, making faith itself, even when it means an action of trust, a work of man by which he earns salvation is equally in error. Or, once more, to suppose that faith, granted it be seen as an action of will and trust, can ever be divorced from obedience in moral behavior is a third misreading of the awesome meaning of justification. When St. James tells us that faith without works is dead, he is not saying that faith *ought* to produce good works. He employs the verb *is*. Subscription to *a* faith, or a system of doctrine, may well require an *ought* for completion. But faith as a personal relationship implies obedience as part of its very self. A trust-relationship without fruitage in response simply *is* dead.

To return, however, to a further wrestling with this haunting paradox of faith. We are to "preach Christ." This means, we are now told, to preach the *work* of Christ—the reconciling act of the Cross, the new covenant "in his blood," the forgiveness of sins. Yet—the question is once again to the fore—if faith is personal trust and commitment, can there be such trust-surrender to a mere event in history, even if this be the atoning miracle of the Cross? "While we were yet sinners, Christ died for us" (Romans 5:8). "God so loved the world that he gave his only-begotten Son" (John 3:16). "For he hath made him to be sin for us, who knew no sin, that we might be made the righteousness of God in him" (II Cor. 5:21). The New Testament rings with such proclamations of the Gospel. But the verbs are in the past tense. Liberalism, in its revolt against the tyranny of *the* faith as assent to intellectualized dogma, at least made us see faith as personal commitment in the present tense. It meant personal allegiance to the human Jesus of the Gospel story. It meant discipleship and imitation and the obedience of moral striving. "If any man will do his will, he shall know the doctrine" (John 7:17). "Blessed are they that hear the word of God, and keep it" (Luke 11:28). "For whosoever shall do the will of God, the same is my brother and my sister, and mother" (Mark 3:35). What happens to this personal religion pictured in the gospels when we submit to the Christianity of dogma of St. Paul and of the early Church?

Analysis of the breakdown of the appealing pre-Resurrection Christianity need not find wearisome repetition here. But its challenge to the Christianity of dogma has as yet not received full and deserved reply. Can it be said, after all, that, when we enter the world of faith of the apostolic era, faith as trust-commitment to the Person of Christ has been replaced by allegiance to an impersonal substitute—even if this be the *work* of Christ and the awesome event of the Atonement? Are the verbs which, to cite Emil Brunner, are the chief words in the recital theology of the Bible in the past tense only?

Such a reading of the Gospel rests, however, upon a failure to follow the drama of the New Testament beyond the recordings of the Synoptic Evangelists. "Accept, we beg you," so the proclaimers of apostolic Christianity could argue, "the dogma of the Incarnation as a clue to the plot of the drama, even if only as a possibility of belief, and then read on, through the Acts of the Apostles, the Epistles, and all. The drama of the New Testament does not end with the recognition scenes of the Resurrection, nor with the Ascension. Pentecost follows and the emergence in history of the Christian Church. This, too, is the *work* of Christ, final resultant of the atoning Cross. It may possibly quite rightly be called the mightiest of the mighty acts of God." "For the Church the world was made," exclaims an early Christian writer.[10]

But can the emergence in history of the Church, if it, too, is only the work of Christ, finally solve the problem of faith as present personal commitment? An answer to this question will be ventured in the next chapter.

[10] *Shepherd of Hermas*, II, 4:1.

CHAPTER V

The Pulpit, the Font, and the Altar

Faith, so the argument of the previous chapter has run, is personal commitment. Liberalism, emancipating itself from dogma, tried to anchor this act of allegiance in the remembered Jesus of history, in discipleship of a Master, and in imitation of the Founder of Christianity as a kind of First Christian. The attempt failed. This Jesus becomes, in the final view, either a sentimentalized ideal or an offense to human pride. It is the work of Christ as Son of God and Saviour, the Atonement through the Cross, and the new covenant in His blood which is the authentic New Testament Gospel.

The Holy Spirit

But, to repeat now the question asked earlier, can even the most moving vision of a relationship or covenant suffice to win us to surrender? As a prospective convert, I am told to repent as a confessed sinner, to believe in the forgiveness of sins, and to enter by faith into the new life of a forgiven prodigal son—all this made possible by an event in the distant past. What has happened to the Person of Christ in this gospel of His atoning work? Has He vanished from the scene, departing to the heavens, leaving His followers to work out on their own their salvation in repentance and surrender of will? Can faith in the legal bond of the marriage covenant, to cite an analogy, take the place of trusting surrender to a living person, the very essence of the marriage relationship resting upon that surrender? The message of the Cross as past event in history may evoke the confession of the Apostles' Creed: I believe in "the forgiveness of sins." Yet the word "forgiveness" is still something of an abstraction. When presented in the context of atonement theologies, with their complicated theories of "sacrifice, oblation, and satisfaction," even a gospel of forgiveness may be obscured behind a veil of doctrinal puzzles. Personal encounter with Christ Himself must come to the rescue.

The climax of the Gospel, however, is that He *does* meet us in personal encounter in the fellowship of the Holy Spirit. He meets us in the Church. His own prophecies are there fulfilled. "Where two or three are gathered in my name, there am I in the midst of them" (Matthew 18:20, RSV). "It is to your advantage that I go away, for if I do not go away, the Comforter will not come unto you." "He shall take of mine, and shall declare it unto you." "I will not leave you desolate; I will come to you" (John, 16:7, RSV; 16:14; 14:18).

Here at last, in the life of the fellowship of the Holy

Spirit, the paradox of faith and *the* faith, as also the paradox of past and present, and that of the Person of Christ and His work, find joyous solution. "I believe in the Holy Ghost: The holy Catholic Church"—this final confession of the historic creeds binds together all that precedes in a living contemporary relationship.

The doctrine of the Trinity—as doctrine in abstraction—remains, one may safely conjecture, a puzzle to the average Christian layman. Yet without the full series of events of the drama of redemption, which the doctrine of the Trinity symbolizes, there could be no Gospel at all. We are to preach Christ and Him crucified. This implies personal encounter, surely. But personal encounter with a departed Master, we have seen, is not really possible. The heart cries out for a *living* God, a *living* Christ. Place Him among the departed immortals, even as one "sitting at the right hand of God," and the gulf between Deity and ourselves is still unbridged. A Christ *now*, a Jesus *now*—no other Christ will win the stubborn heart of man to faith surrender.

A Christ *now* is the climactic proclamation of the Gospel. He is living Lord in His Church—His Body, no less. He has, as it were, once more left His heavenly abode and "emptied himself, taking the form of a servant," and is dwelling among us as the Comforter, the Holy Spirit. Language and symbol break under the burden of expressing the mystery. Christian experience comes to the rescue, since it was the matrix in which the scandal of a belief in "One God in Three Persons" did once arise. We enter here the inner shrine of the mystery of the new life "in Christ," which is the final resultant of the Gospel of Cross and Resurrection and without which the earlier acts of the drama of redemption would lose their meaning. Since life "in the Spirit" has, for many modern Christians, remained an unexplored shrine at the center of the temple of faith, the power of the Gospel has been frequently hidden from sight.

To take seriously the New Testament witness on the presence in the Church of the Holy Spirit as Third Person of the Trinity and, therefore, a revelation of God on an equality with the revelation brought by the Son is, at first, strangely disturbing. "We are inclined," so says a recent report of rediscovery of the authentic New Testament drama, "to establish this difference between the coming of Christ and the coming of the Spirit, that the first is manifest whilst the second is hidden. Such is not original Christian thinking. According to apostolic language, it is Christ who hides after He accomplished His work here on earth, and it is the Spirit who is made manifest. The Spirit is the true theophany after Christ's ascension till the Lord returns again from heaven in the glory of the Father." [1]

[1] In *The Spirit and the Bride*, by Dom Anscar Vonier, a leading exponent of the Liturgical Movement in England (Newman Press, 1935), p. 14. Used by permission of the publisher.

Yet the Christian experience of apostolic days and of the Communion of Saints ever since will surely validate this insight into the drama of God's mighty acts. Imprison Christ as "historic Jesus" in the museum of memory, and He fades into the backdrop of Judea and Galilee. Accept Him as living Lord, risen from the dead and present as Holy Spirit with His people on earth, and He breaks out of the prison house of past event and meets us today on city street or village square. Trinitarian formulae—necessary as guardians against heresy —should not hide from us the breath-taking wonder of apostolic proclamation. The equality that exists between the Persons of the Trinity is as important as the distinctions expressed in the threefold Name. "The Lord is the Spirit," boldly declares St. Paul (II Cor. 3:17). Nor are these two terms the only ones to be joined by an equal sign. The "Spirit" = "in Christ" = "New-Covenant-Life" [2] = "the Church" is the full equation. The Church, in Kierkegaard's words, is "a parenthesis in Christ's life," or "Christ's life on earth." [3] We plumb depth upon depth of meaning when me make our own the phrase that is the thematic refrain of St. Paul's epistles: the jewel-phrase, "in Christ." For "in Christ" = "in the Church" = "in the Spirit" = the "New-Covenant-Life" = the New "Testament."

[2] I borrow this stylistically awkward, but theologically happy phrase, which will appear frequently in following paragraphs, from *Jew and Greek: A Study in the Primitive Church,* by Dom Gregory Dix (London: Dacre Press, 1953), p. 59.

[3] S. Kierkegaard, *Training in Christianity,* translated by Walter Lowrie (London: Oxford University Press, 1941), p. 198.

The Doctrine of the Church

Is it surprising, therefore, that as our day is seeing the end of wilderness wandering in the desert wastes of the Pelagian heresy, the Church is looming large once more in the evangelizing proclamation of the Gospel? The familiar formula on the lips of the revival preacher has been the invitation to "accept Christ." In the era of biblical pietism this invitation could, perhaps, still symbolize the full, or nearly full, Gospel message—the theology of Cross and Resurrection and of incorporation in the New-Covenant-Life. But can it carry that burden of meaning today? Confront the lapsed layman, let alone the man outside the Church, with the Christ-name, and plead for acceptance or submission, will it connote more than an invitation to moral discipleship of a vaguely known religious hero and to imitation of his example?

The word discipleship has received analysis in an earlier chapter. We meet it once more now toward the end of our voyage. If anchored in the sole context of memory of the pre-Resurrection Jesus of history, and then *taken seriously,* this "gospel" of discipleship can lead to nothing except despair, or to a conscience burdened with failure. Unredeemed man is forced to rebellion—to the murder of such a taskmaster. Our contemporary psychiatrists are wrestling with such "murderers of God" in large numbers. And merely to accord Jesus traditional titles of divinity does not help either.

The demand for ethical perfection becomes infinite. "Be ye therefore perfect, even as your father which is in heaven is perfect" (Matthew 5:48). Only in a context in which the revelation of the God of the Old Testament was forgotten or ignored, and God reduced to a human ideal or the custodian of a legal code could such a command be other than an offense to the Pharisee and a call to repentance to the publican. Clearly, it cannot be interpreted as cancelling out the good news that it is precisely "publicans and harlots"— at the opposite pole from perfection—who, by repentance, enter the kingdom before the righteous. This climactic verse of the Sermon on the Mount brings man into court before the ultimate holiness of God, robbing Pharisee and publican alike of pride in self-salvation. Man can respond in only one of two ways: "Crucify Him," or "God be merciful to me, a sinner."

But offense becomes grace, and an imperative becomes an indicative, an *ought* is transformed into an *is*, when we enter the New-Covenant-Life with its gift of the Holy Spirit. A new creature is born who, marvel of marvels, actually imitates Christ. The Epistle to the Ephesians (5:1 ASV) even bids us: "Be ye therefore imitators of *God*." Publicans and sinners, brought to despair of themselves when confronted by Christ as demand, are resurrected from the dead—risen with Christ and sitting with Him in heavenly places. This is discipleship indeed, but a discipleship differing in kind from that of proud moral self-salvation.

True Discipleship

So novel is the mystery of the New-Covenant-Life that St. Paul finds no better way of describing it than as life *"in* Christ." This is New Testament discipleship. The two words are so familiar to us that they no longer shock or surprise. Yet where in all religious speech is there a real parallel? Could a disciple of Socrates have ventured upon such a phrase to describe his relationship to his master—*in* Socrates? Or a follower of Mohammed, or of any of even the most honored heroes of humanity?

And this Christ, into whom the Christian believer is incorporated, is none other than Christ in His Church. He is there as Paraclete or Comforter, as Holy Spirit. Discipleship, accordingly, is churchmanship—the brotherhood becoming, as it were, our Galilee and our Jerusalem, where we are privileged to companion with the Lord of life. Where else can He be met today in truly personal encounter? Where else than where two or three are gathered in His name and He appears in the midst of them, can the publican and sinner receive the courage for a meeting with the holy God of the Bible? We are to preach Christ and Him crucified. We are to bring publican and pharisee into personal encounter with the Second Person of the Trinity, Son of God, Saviour of the world. We may have attempted to mediate this encounter by vivid portrayal of His life here on earth, or even of the redemption wrought for us on the Cross. And this is well. Without memory of

what He once was as Incarnate Word, encounter with
Him in the present would be encounter with a stranger.
But unless memorial leads to a meeting with Christ as
living Lord *now,* discipleship, accepted seriously, can
be a voyage into the loneliness of despair.

To equate discipleship and churchmanship may seem
at first sight a cheapening or secularizing of the Gospel
to the point of absurdity. The Church, as most of us
know it, is very far from being a model of Christlikeness.
It is, of course, the institution in which we hear the
Gospel proclaimed and in which discipleship is laid
upon our conscience. But, apart from serving this function, the Church, as communal witness to the Gospel, is
often thought of as merely the social resultant of discipleship, not as its essential source of power. The whole
weight of the individualism inculcated by pietism—
in Protestantism at least, though Catholicism is guilty
also—protests against churchmanship as being in itself
the imitation of Christ. The very word "churchmanship" needs rescue from secularization and from its
degradation, in some churches at least, to describe di-
visiveness in our midst in place of unity. It ought to
mean the brotherliness of forgiven and forgiving prodigal sons in the Father's redeemed household. In New
Testament language, life "in Christ" is quite literally
life in the Fellowship of the Holy Spirit, and this is,
quite literally again, the Church. Hence it is only in
this brotherhood that Christ can now be met as living
and present Lord and Saviour, and discipleship can have

no other anchorage than when it is the flowering in action of the New-Covenant-Life. This, in turn, is none other than the communal life of the people of God, the Church.

"The central sphere for the working of the exalted Redeemer," so reads a once honored textbook on Christian Ethics, "is the Church, and admission to discipleship takes place by baptism. No one can follow Christ's example, except he who by faith has found Christ as Mediator and Redeemer, and by His saving grace is armed with power to set forth on the pilgrimage after His example." [4] Or, to cite a key verse of the New Testament on the imitation of Christ (I John 2:5,6, RSV): "By this we may be sure that we are in him: he who says he *abides* in him ought to *walk* in the same way in which he walked." The prerequisite for imitation, here again, is the abiding in Christ. If we follow this clue to the meaning of discipleship and imitation through the New Testament, we meet throughout the "scandal" of "churchmanship," even that of the sacraments. Baptism itself is the essential act—not discipleship first, and then the Church as product and result. The reverse is the true order. There must be a dying and a resurrection together with the emergence of a "new creature" (II Cor. 5:17), and an incorporation *into* Christ—the Church, no less—before imitation of Christ becomes a possibility. "Do you not know," says

[4] H. Martensen (Lutheran Bishop of Zealand), *Christian Ethics.* Translated by C. Spence (Edinburgh: T. & T. Clark, 1888), pp. 286 and 293.

St. Paul (Romans 6:3,4, RSV), "that all of us who have been baptized into Christ Jesus were baptized into his death? We were buried therefore with him by baptism into death so that as Christ was raised from the dead by the glory of the Father, *we too might walk in newness of life.*"

The Church a Mystery

Despite the sinful state of its members or even the corporate "grieving of the Holy Spirit" (Ephesians 4:30), which can be so climactic as to provoke God to spew a local manifestation of it out of His mouth (Rev. 3:16), there dwells within the Church the New-Covenant-Life. In other words, Christ is there, even when hidden like a treasure in a seemingly barren field. A covenant or relationship—the marriage covenant can serve here as an analogy—is not destroyed when those who are held in its embrace fail to obey fully its demands or when it places them under awesome judgment. "Take not thy Holy Spirit from us" is the daily prayer of the Church, and we may be confident that God answers this prayer. The New-Covenant-Life of the Gospel is not dependent for its being upon the moral perfection of the members of the Church. It is a gift, not a reward. Response by way of showing forth gratitude for the gift must, of course, be "not only with our lips but in our lives," but performance is not a *pre*requisite for entrance into the Covenant-Life, nor even for restoration when it has been violated. An act of repentance, the prayer "God be merciful to me a sinner," can restore the covenant relationship with all its original wonder and joy. The New-Covenant-Life, which is Christ Himself, is clearly not to be primarily or exclusively identified with the perfection of our moral response, since this Life is the active power—the "dynamism" (Ephesians 1:19) —that evokes that response and motivates it in action.

Many of us will, I suspect, shrink from giving to the Church a place in the proclamation of the Gospel that is fully equal with that of the remembered Jesus as Master and of the good news of the Cross. The Cross, to go no further, is already a sufficient "scandal" and "stumbling-block" (I Cor. 1:23), yet the Cross was God's doing and can claim perfection. Our presenting the Church as climax of the Gospel forces *us*, to be sure, out upon the stage. But are we good news? Are we living embodiments of Christ? Are we the Gospel? "The mystery of the Church," says a recent writer "is deeper still, if that were possible, than the mystery of Christ, just as that mystery was more difficult to believe than the mystery of God, a 'scandal' not only to Jews, but also to many Christians." [5]

Yet we in our age of depersonalized individualism may have to rediscover the Church as Gospel and place it in the forefront of our preaching. As the Church of the first four centuries had to wrestle out the theology

[5] Henri De Lubac, *Catholicism* (New York: Longmans, Green & Co., 1950), p. 28.

of the Second Person of the Trinity, our era may be called upon to rediscover and to bring to life the theology of the Third Person, the Holy Spirit.

I would call to witness in behalf of this conviction the emerging consensus of those who, in our time, are pioneers in evangelism. One such pioneer, George McLeod, becoming known throughout our Christian world as the founder of the Iona Community in Scotland, one of the outstanding experiments in "Church evangelism," pictures our contemporary dilemma thus:

The fundamental reason why the Christian message fails to get across is that those who expound it assume that Christendom still exists, whereas in reality it has disappeared. One set of orders was needed for a time when Christians were like an army billeted in every home in the land. A quite different set of orders is required when the Church is in fact withdrawn into hedge-hog positions in a vast waste of incomprehension and of alien thought forms. This means that the traditional order in presenting the Gospel needs to be reversed. The prevailing practice is to start from God the Creator, tell men of the redemptive work of Christ, and lead them by this path into the experience of the fellowship of the Holy Spirit. But since the content of our message has ceased to have any meaning for them, the only thing to be done is to begin at the other end by showing them community in actual operation. Something new must enter into their experience before they can understand the Christian message.[6]

This insight must look, at first sight, like turning the

[6] Quoted in *The Christian News Letter* (London), March 6, 1946. Used by permission of the publisher.

traditional Trinitarian faith of Christianity topsy-turvy or upside down. Yet, if taken seriously, experience may validate it. Its implications for the preaching ministry are profound. It may turn out to be the salvation of the evangelizing vocation of the Church for our time.

Churchmanship

To catch a glimpse of what the Gospel as churchmanship can mean in terms of living experience, we may well return, for a moment, to the theme of the previous chapter—faith. We, the proclaimers of the Gospel, are to win men through their act of faith surrender to the God of biblical revelation. This means the capitulation of the citadel of man's pride. It means the broken and the contrite heart. It places the Pharisee on the same plane as the publican and harlot. It means the strait gate and the narrow way—not of moral self-culture, but of repentance. It means imitation of Christ in His death, the dying symbolized by the drowning flood waters of baptism. Is this a simple demand, easily met by way of a few New Year's resolutions, or response to a pulpit homily on moral reform, or resolves, however well meant, to lead a better life? "For the Gentiles seek all these things" (Matthew 6:32). The Stoic philosopher and the secular idealist, and even the disciple of Karl Marx, can produce examples of self-sacrifice and of moral heroism that leave most of us far behind. The New-Covenant-Life in Christ demands rebirth and the emergence of a "new creature" (II Cor. 6:17), the Church being the "mother" at whose breast the new-born child of the covenant receives its nurture (Gal. 4:26). The difference between a Christian convert and the Stoic moral hero, or the disciplined Buddhist, or the Confucian sage, or the cultured secular humanist, does not consist first of all in the ethical perfection of the Christian as over against that of his rivals. The latter may be veterans of moral discipline, the Christian a child in arms, taking his first steps on the pathway of discipleship "in Christ." The decisive difference is between the lost and the found, between entrance into eternal life and wandering in the desert wastes of idolatry.

The Church or—to avoid the inevitable ambiguity of the word—the New-Covenant-Life of which the Church is outward and visible sacrament, must, if New Testament guidance is accepted, be seen again as the prime agent of evangelism. Churchmanship is integral to the Gospel. Christ must be met as living Lord, as the power of the Holy Spirit, or there can be no death of the sinner and no resurrection. *Extra ecclesiam nulla salus*—outside the fellowship of the repentant and forgiven no salvation! "If any man have not the Spirit of Christ, he is none of his" (Rom. 8:9). "Hereby know ye that we dwell in him, and he in us, because he hath given us of his Spirit" (I John 4:13). And the Spirit is Christ in his Body, the Church. Scandal though it be, personal encounter with Christ means meeting Him in the brotherhood of fellow sinners. The trust-surrender of faith is a suicide action, impossible for man except through the power of Christ Himself. The community of faith can alone mediate that power—"the immeasurable greatness of his power *in us who believe*" (Ephesians 1:19).

The wheel of the Gospel, if the figure be allowed, comes full circle. We are to preach Christ, so runs our hallowed refrain. But Christomonism, especially if it is a mere Jesus-monism, is not yet the full Gospel. As the ancient Athanasian Creed boldly reminds us: "The Father is God, the Son is God: and the Holy Ghost is God. And yet they are not three Gods: but one God." The God of faith must be the triune God. The trust act of faith must be ultimately a surrender to God the Father, *through* the Son, and *in* the fellowship of the Holy Spirit.

The Spirit as Power

Will acceptance of such a version of a fully Trinitarian Gospel affect our preaching? Clearly, it dare not belittle the proclamation of the good news of God's mighty act of redemption in Christ as a past event—the "once for all" of Incarnation, Cross, and Resurrection —nor the story of the Word becoming flesh and dwelling among us, full of grace and truth. "How shall they believe in him of whom they have not heard?" (Rom. 10:14) Nothing can take the place of the recital the-

ology of the Bible. Yet this proclamation of the creation
by divine act of the New-Covenant-Life is still only
good news *about* grace. It can woo and invite and move
heart and will. But until grace appears, not only as
promise but as power, and until the repentant sinner is
incorporated *into* Christ, being reborn and made a new
creature, the Gospel remains merely verbalized vision—
at times, a mere mirage. The convert sets out on his
lonely journey of discipleship and, when failure ensues,
his last state may be worse than his first. The Gospel
has become one of unbearable demand.

An analogy may be helpful. Few groups dedicated to
the vocation of social redemption are more conspicuous
on the American scene than Alcoholics Anonymous.
Often active under the sponsorship of a church, though
tangential to the Church's own ministry, "AA," as it is
commonly known, can furnish object lessons to its
"mother" institution. The steps by which redemption
is opened to the victim of strong drink are familiar.
They parallel in a striking manner the road which the
Christian convert is asked to travel—despair of self-
salvation, the good news of possible redemption in a
fellowship of brethren in weakness, the confession of
helplessness and need of grace ("I am John Doe; I am
a drunk!"), the embrace of the "prodigal" by the brotherhood, and then the new life motivated by gratitude
for such undeserved acceptance and continued in the
strength of the corporate "esprit de corps." When applied to the Church, the analogy is, of course, incom-

plete. It excerpts, as it were, the human half of the New-Covenant-Life of the Church, and an observer could well ask how long Alcoholics Anonymous would retain its powers of redemption were it to wander far from its orbit as satellite of the fellowship of the *Holy* Spirit. Yet for the purpose of clarifying the place of churchmanship in evangelism, the analogy, clearly, has much to teach us. The preceding argument has been wrestling with the relative value to be accorded to verbal proclamation of the Gospel as compared with that Gospel in action in the sacramental incorporation of the convert into Christ and his nurture in the Church. The evangelizing vocation of Alcoholics Anonymous includes verbal proclamation also. The prospective convert must hear the good news of possible redemption. The drama of death and resurrection—death of trust in self and resurrection as a new creature in the brotherhood—will come to him first as a story told, a gospel in word. Hope must be born in his heart and trust in the witnessing missioner, leading up to the venture of faith. But the final agent of redemption is the power residing in the corporate group itself.

The evaluation of the relative importance of the Gospel as a verbal proclamation compared with the Gospel as a *power alive* in the corporate life of the Church herself may well have received distortion in the analogy just employed. Yet a fair remnant of insight has, I trust, received underscoring. The Christ whom we preach must be Christ in His Church, as well as the Christ of memory and of the "once for all" mighty acts of Cross and Resurrection. He is the ascended Christ, coming again to judge the living and the dead, but also present in His Body now. The Church, sacrament of the New-Covenant-Life of the Spirit, is herself the chief agent of evangelism.

Preaching to the Church

Has this insight, to repeat our question, meaning for our preaching? Clearly, it can stand in judgment over some at least of our pulpit ambitions. How tempting it has been to preach to the world *from* the Church, to berate it for its sins, or to flatter it for its virtues. Or, if we have realized the futility of addressing an audience not present in our pews (even when Monday's news-paper quotes our purpled rhetoric), we may still remain blind to our primary calling, the nurture of the New-Covenant-Life within the sanctuary where we stand.

Peter Taylor Forsyth, hailed as a prophet for our time in an earlier chapter, has wise counsel on this issue also. Is a minister's first duty to his Church or to the world? In reply to this question, he answers:

If we must choose in what is perhaps a false dilemma, it is to his Church. The duty to the world is a joint duty of preacher and Church . . . It is part of the price we pay for popular preachers that we fall into a way of think-ing as if, when a gifted speaker appears, the main duty of the Church is to give him his platform, or even his pedestal, and then to stand out of his way. Hence manifold mischief to preacher, Church, and Gospel; the cossetting of the preacher's self-will, the elimination of the communal will, the deflection of the will of God. The task of the great preacher is at bottom the task of the smaller preacher who can but be faithful. It is to act upon the world through his Church and not merely *from* his Church. His Church is not the arena for his individualism (far less the pedestal of his vanity) but its school. The captive of the Gospel will never lord it in the Lord's house, nor use the flock he is there to feed.[7]

This is humbling counsel, and the natural man within us resents its implications. We look back upon the era of the great preacher, in the century or more just past, with envy. There are, so many contemporary observers would report, not many such preachers left. But if we take seriously the diagnosis of our situation today as one in which Christendom, as an embracing environment, has vanished (I refer to the words of George McLeod already quoted), we may envision our vocation in our time to be more modest in outward show, but no less important or blessed of God. A vacuum has appeared; Christendom is no longer an embracing environment. The great preacher may well have to stand aside until we, the "smaller preachers" of the Church, have filled the vacuum with a revived community of Spirit power. If Christ can no longer be proclaimed as a living Christ in His Church, He cannot be proclaimed at all.

[7] P. T. Forsyth, *Positive Preaching and the Modern Mind* (London: The Independent Press, third edition, 1949), pp. 72-3. Used by permission of the publisher.

The Church under Judgment

The Survey on Evangelism presented for discussion to the Second Assembly of the World Council of Churches (Evanston, 1954) rings almost monotonous changes on the cry for a revived New-Covenant-Life within the churches as the first requisite, if the Gospel is to be heard by men and women in our time. "Most reports," so the Survey summarizes the harvest of confessions, "start off with an extensive section entitled, 'What is wrong with the Church?' Unsuccessful communication is explained more readily in terms of the scandal of the Church than in terms of the hardening of hearts by those outside." Or, again: "Evangelism should be conceived in terms of the impact of the Christian Community on its total environment. Very definitely the general trend is away from considering evangelism as a specialized activity performed by a few specialists. Our need is not so much for more evangelists, but for an evangelizing Church." "There is ample evidence that *individualism* in its varied forms is definitely on the decrease in evangelistic thinking. The agent of evangelism is seen in a representative capacity. Even if he be a single person, he is part of a corporate personality and he is thought of as the nucleus of an anticipated community." "Total evangelism can be nothing short of a convincing, corporate demonstration by the whole Laos (the people of the Mission) of Christ's solidarity with mankind." "The Church itself must be the true means of evangelism and to that end the Church must be born again." "Mass methods of evangelism"—this confession coming from a European report—"have in the past depended on the presumed existence of a Christian community as a reality to which the lapsed may be recalled or into which the converted may be brought. It is necessary to face the fact that such a community does not exist at all among the people with whom the Church is concerned." "Theological reflection has elucidated that 'witness' can never be reduced to a *verbal* proclamation. Biblical witness happens simultaneously through proclamation (*kerygma*), fellowship (*koinonia*), and service (*diakonia*). The life witness of the entire community encompasses and qualifies every spoken word." "Your community speaks so loud that we cannot hear your words." "The spiritual poverty and unpreparedness of the Church is such that no one can desire that a large number of those now outside should enter the churches as they are." [8]

These honest contemporary reports contain severe, if not devastating, indictments. And the pulpit, surely, must shoulder at least part of the blame. How tempting it has been, to echo Forsyth's epigram once more, to preach *from* the Church, instead of *to* the Church.

[8] *Evangelism—the Mission of the Church to Those Outside her Life*. An Ecumenical Survey. In *Six Ecumenical Surveys* (New York: Harper and Brothers, 1954), pp. 52, 55, 54, 28, 57, and 58. The last quotation is taken from *Evangelization of Modern Man in Mass Society,* a World Council of Churches pamphlet (October, 1949), p. 12.

Who, to prove by example, has not preached a sermon against racial prejudice or against many another social sin of our time? But what about preparing our flock for becoming a non-segregated fellowship next week or next month? Or for paying back the debt owed to God's larger human family incurred when our caste-conscious parish fled the city's depressed area to a refuge in pleasant suburbia? And these are but surface illustrations of what preaching *to* the Church may involve. There are those within the Church's ministerial order called upon to preach the Gospel in the market place, as did St. Paul on the Athenian Areopagus, and well may the Church support them in their missionary vocation. Yet this was not St. Paul's normal exercise of the ministry of the Word, nor, for most of us, should it be ours. St. Paul's homiletic gifts were poured into his letter-sermons to the households of the faith. And we may be certain that, so far as ease of composition was concerned, he would gladly have prepared a score of lectures on the "unknown God" if he could have been spared the letters to the Church of Corinth. The Epistle to the Ephesians defines "the work of ministry" as "building up the body of Christ, until we all attain to the unity of the faith and of the knowledge of the Son of God" (Ephesians 4:12,13). In other words, if the Body of Christ becomes mature of stature and upbuilded in love (Ephesians 4:13,16), Christ in His Church and through His Church will be His own evangelist.

The Sacraments

A "reborn Church" is evangelism's cry today. Can the contemporary pulpit meet the demand? One test of a truly reborn Church, if the New Testament *ecclesia* serves as pattern, will appear, at first, like a lowering of the pulpit's long time monopoly of honor over font and altar, since, in many areas of Protestant church life, it will mean a revival of the sacraments. That the pulpit, in recent generations at least, has yielded to monopolistic temptations is confessed today by many observers. Ernst Troeltsch, noted Church historian, speaks of the "dying of the sacraments" on Protestant soil, and Paul Tillich (again, not a prejudiced Catholic spokesman) declares that Protestantism has never yet solved the problem of how, in its resistance to the sacerdotally monopolized cultus of Rome, it can avoid yielding to secularism. "This resistance has attained such dimensions that the Cult has almost become a hidden-in-the-corner affair." [9] Baptism, to mention the most conspicuous example (a scandal some would call it), has, at least in churches in which it is normally administered to children, frequently become little more than a private family rite whose chief value lies in its guarantee of social respectability. And the eucharist, or Lord's Supper (even when the problem of frequency or infrequency is not made an issue) has

[9] A translated passage from Paul Tillich's essay, *Natur und Sakrament*, in *Religioese Verwirklichung* (Berlin: Furche Verlag 1929), p. 61.

become, for many otherwise loyal church members, an
archaic memorial ordinance, honored in observance, but
only vaguely understood, and, compared with the sermon, of quite minor importance. Yet a Church without
the sacraments, or with neglected sacramental unity, is
not the *ecclesia* of the New Testament norm. Even a
secular social group knows better than to ignore its
"sacramental" means of preserving its organic life. (The
Rotary or Kiwanis luncheon, with disciplined attendance, could be one of many examples.) Baptism, in the
New Testament, is a realistic incorporation into the
Body of Christ, a dying and rising again, prerequisite
for receiving the gifts of the Spirit. The Lord's Supper,
proclaiming "the Lord's death till he come" (I Cor.
11:26), is the corporate self-offering of the fellowship
and a becoming one in Christ, a requisite, in its turn,
for renewal of the Body of Christ's unity and power.
The Body of Christ is something more than a genial
sociality. It is a divine, not a human creation. It must
meet at the *Lord's* table, as well as at that table which
we spread for one another.

The pulpit, clearly, dare not lord it over font and
altar. It must imitate the pulpit's Master and be servant
of the New-Covenant-Life, and not become an indi-
vidualized substitute for it. Pulpit sacerdotalism may
be as much a deflection of the New Testament pattern
of the ministry as the sacerdotalism of the altar of
which the Protestant accuses Rome. The true minister
as servant may well walk at the head of his flock, but

he will not act in its stead. The Church, not the lone minister, is to be Christ to the world. But the surrender of its monopolist honors, far from lessening the pulpit's vocation, brings to it its true glory. Is nurturing the Bride of Christ, to be "presented before him in splendor, without spot of wrinkle or any such thing" (Eph. 5:27)—the Lord's Supper, the sacramental marriage feast—a belittled vocation?

Baptism and the Lord's Supper

Nor need the revival of the sacramental life of the Church mean substituting for the proclamation of the Gospel lectures on liturgics or on cultic rubrics. Clearly, the theology of baptism goes to the very heart of the Gospel itself—rebirth, the imitation of Christ in His death and participation in His resurrection, as, indeed, in the whole drama of the New-Covenant-Life in Christ. In most of our churches (the Baptist communions avoiding this handicap), the preacher will have before him Church members christened in infancy, scarcely conscious, even on the testimony of their elders, of its awesome meaning. What an opportunity to proclaim to them the good news of what they already are by unmerited grace—members of Christ and inheritors of the kingdom of heaven! But it will be proclamation of a grace that is, at the same time, a judgment. Dare membership in the Body of Christ—of Him who is coming to judge the living and the dead—be taken

lightly? Shall the Church of Rome have a monopoly
of the insight that wilful neglect of church attendance
is a grieving of the Holy Spirit? "When thou teachest,"
so reads an early Church document, "command the
people that they be constant in the assembly of the
Church; so that ye be not hindered and make smaller
by a member the Body of Christ. Do not deprive our
Savior of His members; do not mangle or scatter His
Body." [10]

The theology of the eucharist, or Lord's Supper, to
touch on this briefly in its turn, can highlight once
more the memorial of the mighty acts of the drama of
redemption, but even more Christ's presence *now* in
His Body, empowering it for its work in the world. The
liturgical movement, spreading out from the Benedic-
tines of Romanist allegiance into virtually all Christian
communions, furnishes a host of insights into the New-
Covenant-Life of the people of God, which, if proclaimed and received, can prepare for the coming of
the "reborn Church." Here, in this mystery, the "remembered Christ" reveals Himself as at the same time
the present Lord, amazing the pharisees in our midst
by receiving sinners and eating with them (Luke 15:2).
"When the Church celebrates the Eucharistic mysteries"—I venture to cite one insight out of a multitude
which the revival of sacramental theology in our time
stands ready to give us—"she does not stretch forth to

[10] *Didascalia,* chapter 13. Quoted by W. J. Phythian-Adams, in
The Church Quarterly Review, June, 1943.

the unseen regions of heaven; she is not laying hands on a distant Bridegroom; she sends forth no piercing cry to call Him down from the skies; on the contrary . . . she becomes conscious of a presence that was there potentially all the time; she speaks phrases and performs actions that are more like the monologues of a person full of joy than conversations with an outsider, with a stranger." [11]

One who is deeply anchored in Protestant loyalities and reads the plea we make here for "preaching the sacraments" may suspect it of Catholicising propaganda. But it must run that risk. Yet, if the cry today of pioneers in evangelism for the "reborn Church" is a voice of the Spirit speaking to the churches (Rev. 1:22), then, surely, exploring the riches of God's witness to Himself in the two-thirds of Christendom on the other side of the Protestant-Catholic gulf may not be out of place. Nor need this exploration belittle in the slightest the pulpit's own authority—gloriously revived in the churches of the Reformation. It is precisely by way of the ministry of the Word that font and altar will again become, for churches that have forgotten their meaning, thrilling means of grace. Baptism and the Lord's Supper simply *are* integral to the Gospel. The last command of Jesus to His disciples,

[11] Dom Anscar Vonier, *The Spirit and the Bride* (Newman Press, 1935), pp. 226-27. Used by permission of the publisher. The quotation could be read in connection with the passage by the same author cited earlier (page 131) on the Holy Spirit as the true "theophany" after Christ's Ascension.

as the first Evangelist of our New Testament reports it, lays both upon our conscience, baptism by name and the fellowship of the Supper by implication: "Go ye therefore and make disciples of all nations, baptizing them . . . and lo, I am with you always" (Matthew 28:19-20).

Servant of the Word

Nor, against the background of the plea that a minister's first duty is *to* his Church, will the authority of the pulpit suffer damage. The preacher is servant of his Church, but he is also servant of the Word, and never more servant of his Church than when faithful servant of the Word. Christ is Christ for us today only if He is recognized as Christ in His Church, the Spirit the true theophany after His departure "to prepare a place" for us until He comes again to receive us unto Himself (John 14:2-3). But He remains the Church's Head and Lord. The Church is sacrament of the kingdom, not yet its consummation. It is Bride, and not Bridegroom. It can become again, as did the people of the covenant in the days of Hosea, a harlot. As servant of the Word, the preacher must bear the burden of voicing words of the Lord *against* His Church, as well as the words that assure his flock that they are even now "kings and priests" (Rev. 1:6). In forgetting that Christ retains crown rights in His kingdom, and thus in divinizing herself, the proud Church of the papacy had to see rising up against her in judgment, in the days of the Reformers, the ministry of the Word. But this ministry, it is well for Protestantism to remember, was itself nurtured within the bosom of the same Church which it called to repentance. Gospel and Fellowship of the Holy Spirit, Bible and Church belong together.

Indeed, so deeply are Church and sacraments integral to the Gospel itself, when seen in its full orb of wonder and grace, that a loyal return of the pulpit to biblical theology must itself prepare the way for the "reborn Church." Let us, the proclaimers of the Gospel, ministers of the awesome Word of God, heed the call to a return to expository preaching, and we may well find that we have heard "the conclusion of the whole matter" (Eccles. 12:13). How humble it seems—this opening of the Bible and making its words and symbols come alive. We may have to forego clever titles for our sermons in our newspaper advertisements—at least when we substitute our man-made epigrams for the sacred texts of Scripture.

The drama of the Bible—recital theology—expository preaching—biblical theology. Any of these could well serve as a motto for the revival, in our time, of theology in the pulpit. And as we and our people hear rightly again the epic of God's mighty acts of redemption, we and they will rediscover that we are actors ourselves in this drama of God's design. We shall be again joyful witnesses, carrying its message of eternal life to the ends of the earth. We have pictured the New-Cove-

nant-Life of the Church as the climactic act. And so it
is by way of foretaste and pledge of even the Last
Things—the consummation which awaits the people
of God when the Christ whom we have preached "shall
come again, with glory, to judge both the quick and
the dead." "Blessed be the God and Father of our Lord
Jesus Christ, who *hath* blessed us with all spiritual
blessings in heavenly places in Christ: According as he
hath chosen us in him before the foundation of the
world . . ." (Eph. 1:3-4).

Yet mention of the Last Things does remind us that
even the life "in Christ" of the Church, though it be
a life in which we have already been raised from the
dead and are sitting together in heavenly places in
Christ Jesus (Eph. 2:6), does look forward to a further mighty act of God—the new heaven and the new
earth on the other side of Judgment Day and of the
"resurrection both of the just and unjust" (Acts 24:15).
The awesome fact of death does still confront even the
Church militant on earth—and even more awesomely
those who have refused the offer of the resurrected life
of the repentant and the forgiven. Confronting our
hearers with a decision—fateful for eternity as well as
time—is the final burden of our preaching. Can our era
of theological revival give us help in presenting to our
people the eschatological symbols of the biblical revelation? The closing chapter of our volume will venture to
explore modestly these ultimate mysteries of the Christian faith.

CHAPTER VI

✠ ✠ ✠

The Community of Faith as the Agent of Salvation

William Temple, writing his Gifford Lectures a generation ago, ventured, in a chapter dealing with the Christian doctrines concerning eternal life, the following comment:

Every consideration of serious importance intensifies the urgency of the moral demand for at least a possibility of life after the death of the body. Yet there has never been a period in which there was so little belief in this, or indeed so widespread an absence of concern for the whole subject.[1]

Life after Death

Have the decades since the Archbishop's Gifford lectures wrought a change from unconcern to renewed interest in eschatology? Indications are not lacking that such is, indeed, a fact. Books on Christian doctrine dealing with the Last Things are again multiplying on

[1] William Temple, *Nature, Man and God* (London: Macmillan & Company, 1934), p. 453. Used by permission of the publisher.

our library shelves. The choice of the topic of Hope as the main theme for the Second Assembly of the World Council of Churches is in itself a conspicuous theological landmark. The leaders of the ecumenical movement, in their choice of this theme, may have envisaged, at the first, an ecumenical consideration of hope as a general concomitant of Christian faith, but the flood of discourse soon burst such bounds. We are in the midst of stormy expeditions to recover the whole eschatological deposit of Christian doctrine. The sophisticated theologian has converse once more with his fundamentalist brother as he, too, wrestles afresh with such long neglected symbols as the second coming of Christ, judgment day, heaven and hell, death, eternity, and the mystery of time.

My modest essay will not be so bold as to steer its course into this larger whirlpool of debate, though, in matters eschatological, it is true that if you touch one doctrine, you touch all. I limit myself, if delimitation is possible, to what our revived eschatological concern is doing to the doctrine of the Church, the community of faith.

The Medieval View

Every one familiar with the history of Christian doctrine knows that the formula *extra ecclesiam nulla salus* —a classic phrase since the Fourth Lateran Council of

1215, though in substance tracing its lineage back at least to St. Cyprian—is a solidly anchored doctrine in the historic confessions of the churches of Christendom, both Catholic and Protestant (I spare you the voluminous quotations). As background to the doctrine stood an awesome, but intelligible and homiletically powerful, picture map of the world beyond death. Immortality, and even a bodily resurrection (John 5:29 being the key text in the New Testament), is simply assumed. Hell awaits those who are beyond pardon. For those who do merit salvation, Catholic and Protestant schemes offer variant destinies, with purgatory, in the Catholic picturization, being an intermediate state between death and entrance into Paradise, or the ultimate post-resurrection heaven. Judgment, in both schemes, is twofold: the one being an immediate pronouncement of bliss or doom at the soul's departure from the earthly scene, the other the climactic assize at Christ's second coming.

There it stands—the monumental orthodox structure of doctrine concerning life after death. Buttressed with biblical texts as proof, clothed in gorgeous poetry by a Dante and a Milton, enshrined in the classic confessions of the churches, it has dominated the imagination of Christians for well nigh two thousand years. Yet, if contemporary theology is asked whether it can continue unquestioned acceptance of this doctrinal structure, it would have to say "no." Cracks are visible in the scheme in both Catholic and Protestant apologetic.

The Revolt

In the freer atmosphere of Protestantism the revolt against tradition is by many theologians openly acknowledged. Even doctrines of universal salvation, such as that which beclouds the memory of Origen, are seeing a rebirth. But this is still exceptional. Somehow, the terrifying reality of decision for or against God and the symbol of hell are still taken seriously, though softened frequently by a remoulding of portrayals of the intermediate state of a departed soul between death and final judgment. *The Great Divorce,* by C. S. Lewis, and the novels of Charles Williams are popularizing such a modified mythology for English readers. Christian conscience, it is clear, in large areas of contemporary Protestant Christianity, has at last revolted against the portrayal of God as a Judge condemning any one to endless torment with no opportunity for a change of doom by repentance. Surely, so the argument runs, if neither death nor divine judgment destroys the image of God in man or His gift of freedom, then the God known to Christian faith could not be so bound to legalism as to refuse acceptance of a prodigal's return, however long delayed in the ongoing aeons of eternity. Berdyaev, that bold critic of encrusted dogma, yielding to no one in loyal retention of hell as a reality of human experience, solves the dilemma of judgment and grace by assigning hell to the aeon of time and a final victory of salvation to eternity.[2]

To accuse Berdyaev, William Temple, and many other contemporary theologians of outright universalism would be unfair. If possibility of repentance is brought upon the eschatological stage, its opposite is brought there also. "Hell is admissible" says Berdyaev "in the sense that a man may want it and prefer it to paradise. The idea of hell is the expression of an acute and intense experience of the indestructible nature of personality. It is the idea of freedom and not of justice that dialectically presupposes hell." But, at the very least, the dogma of an unalterable pronouncement of endless doom upon an unpardoned soul at death has been surrendered. Even into eternity the Christian must be able to sing:

> There's a wideness in God's mercy
> Like the wideness of the sea.
> There is mercy with the Saviour,
> There is healing in his blood.

[2] See Nicholas Berdyaev, *The Destiny of Man* (London: Geoffrey Bles, 1945), pp. 266-283, a chapter entitled *Hell*. Another typical re-evaluation of traditional doctrine, also opening doors to a possible universalism, is *In the End God*, by John A. T. Robinson (London: James Clarke, 1950). William Temple's similar reinterpretation is found in his Gifford Lectures, cited earlier. A German theologian's critical summary of contemporary eschatological thought is *Die Letzten Dinge*, by Paul Althaus (Gütersloh, 1923).

Two Analogies Contrasted

It appears to the present writer that what has happened in both Protestant and Catholic doctrinal developments is a momentous shift in the analogies in which eschatological doctrine has traditionally been clothed. That anchored in tradition was the juridic analogy—the analogy of the law court. The verdict at death resulting in salvation or damnation was, to be sure, not based solely on an evaluation of ethical achievements or merit. The sinner standing before the bar of judgment could plead justification by grace and faith, and a deathbed repentance could blot out a lifetime of crime. But, the verdict once rendered, inexorable law took charge. The doctors of the schools exhausted their powers of argument in defending the thesis that never ending punishment for the damned did not violate divine love. Could the doctrine of predestination, deeply imbedded in Holy Scripture, lead to any other result?

The fading from the contemporary scene of literalist biblicism and the arrival of historically responsible theology has meant loss, as well as gain. But would many of us wish to return to the vindictive picturization of hell of our forefathers? We can still abandon ourselves to the lure of Dante's *Divine Comedy* when we read it as an epic of a soul's journey from despair to joyous faith; but as a trustworthy map of life beyond death, it has, for our age at least, probably lost its authority.

Contemporary theology has not attempted to read the doctrine of election out of the Bible. But it is a significant fact, surely, that, in its juridic form, symbolized by the doctrine of a double predestination, it has well-nigh vanished from view today even in the Reformed tradition. Bishop Gustav Aulen, in his *The Faith of the Christian Church,* summarizes the result of this theological revolution when he bluntly declares: "The juridical analogies prove inadequate when it is a question of interpreting the inner character of the relationship to God." [3]

To define the analogies which can give new meaning to our traditional eschatological doctrines is not a simple task. A clue, however, is offered in the sentence just quoted from Bishop Aulen—"the inner character of the relationship to God." When we employ analogies of relationship between persons, new perspectives on our timeworn eschatological symbols do emerge. To cite one example at the outset: it is noteworthy that William Temple, in the very chapter in which he presents a devastating criticism of mediaeval eschatology, inserts an argument which brings a realistic fear of hell back upon the scene. Referring to the New Testament and its insistence upon the abiding consequences of our actions, he continues:

[3] Gustav Aulen, *The Faith of the Christian Church* (Philadelphia: The Muhlenberg Press, 1948), p. 290.

Language is strained and all imagery of apocalypse employed to enforce the truth that a child's choice between right and wrong matters more than the courses of the stars. Whatever is done bears fruit for ever; whatever a man does, to all eternity he is the man who did that.[4]

I seem to have wandered far form my announced topic—the Community of Faith as the Agent of Salvation. I still have it in view, I assure you. But I bespeak your patience for a further exposition of the byway already partially explored. It leads, I dare to suggest, directly into a doctrine of the Church.

Existentialist Philosophy

No one familiar with the theological climate of the twentieth century is ignorant of the fact that we are confronted by a radical reorientation brought about by the emergence of existential philosophy and by its challenge to the theologian to wrestle afresh with the problem of relationship between persons. Some of us may even be wearied by now of the uncritical Kierkegaard worshipper or of the "I-Thou" theme of Martin Buber, or have grown faint of heart in trying to master the basic texts of Heidegger or Sartre. But we may be certain that, as Emil Brunner predicts in his recent

[4] William Temple, *op. cit.*, p. 465. Used by permission of the publisher.

Dogmatik, we have barely made a beginning in adjusting our theological world view, inherited from the era of rational scholasticisms, to the depth-dimension yawning before us when we explore the dynamism of personal life, of the "I" in encounter with the "Thou," and of the problem of communication and relationship between these islands of subjective isolation.[5] Karl Heim, in launching his voyages of discovery into this unexplored continent of new insights, hails the discovery in our era of the "I" and the "Thou" as comparable to the Copernican revolution in astronomical science.[6]

One of the insights brought to us by existentialist exploration of personal relationships is of particular importance for a doctrine of the Church. The existentialist philosopher has opened our eyes to the fact of man's loneliness in the universe and of the gulf of separation which exists between person and person, let alone between man and God. Every human being is a mysterious "I," subject, not object. Yet he does not discover himself as a subject except in encounter with other similar centers of consciousness. The person, as a self-conscious "I," is born only in community. Paul Tillich describes this discovery by a man of himself as

[5] Emil Brunner, *The Christian Doctrine of Creation and Redemption—Dogmatics* (Philadelphia: The Westminster Press, 1952), II, v.

[6] Karl Heim, *Christian Faith and Natural Science* (New York: Harper and Brothers, 1953), p. 112.

a person in a passage which embodies much existential-ist insight:

No personal being exists without communal being. The person as the fully developed, individual self is impossible without other developed selves. If he did not meet the resistance of other selves, every self would try to make himself absolute. But the resistance of the other selves is unconditional. One individual can conquer the entire world of objects, but he cannot conquer another person without destroying him as a person. The individual discovers himself through this resistance. If he does not want to destroy the other person, he must enter into communion with him. In the resistance of the other person, the person is born. Therefore, *there is no person without an encounter with other persons.* Persons can grow only in the communion of personal encounter.[7]

This insight, if pursued, involves readjustment in more than one of our traditional theological concepts, especially in those of the Church and of salvation. A traditional view of how community comes to birth is that symbolized by the theory of the social contract—individual first, community second. More than one view of the Church echoes this conviction: a conscious individual conversion is demanded prior to possible incorporation into the community of faith. Are we now asked to accept a reversal of this order of priorities?

[7] Paul Tillich, *Systematic Theology* (Chicago: The University of Chicago Press, 1951), I, pp. 176-77 (italics mine). Copyright 1951 by the University of Chicago. Used by permission of the publisher.

Loneliness

The moment, however, that we do exalt the community as requisite for personal self-discovery, a further paradox confronts us. The person, so the radical existentialist tells us, may, indeed, come to self-realization only in encounter with other persons, but there the process ends. Isolation, not community, is the result. In the eyes of another person, I am an object, not a subject. My world is my world, and it can embrace, by way of spatial imagination, the farthest stars. My freedom is my freedom, and my decisions are my decisions. Place over against me, however, another such center of spatial consciousness, freedom, and mastery over decisions, and two totalitarian universes clash. "Suddenly," so our French contemporary Sartre analyses personal encounter, "an object is presented before me which has stolen my world away from me." [8] Or again: "The essence of the relationships between modes of consciousness is not togetherness, it is conflict." [9] Or still again, to cite the now famous epigram of his drama *No Exit:* "Hell is—other people!" [10]

It is tempting for the Christian to label all this simply atheism and to pass it by. Yet let him look again. This

[8] Quoted in *Existentialist Philosophies,* by Emmanuel Mounier (London: Rockcliff, 1948), p. 76.
[9] J. P. Sartre, *L'Etre et le Ne'ant* (Paris, 1943), p. 502.
[10] J. P. Sartre, *No Exit* (New York: Alfred A. Knopf, 1949), p. 61.

may well be the true picture of the human scene *extra
ecclesiam*—humanity outside the community of grace.
Man is condemned to be free, and must bear his burden
of freedom in loneliness. Matthew Arnold, a century
ago, described our human lot in words prophetic of our
era of disillusionment:

> Yes! in the sea of life enisled,
> With echoing straits between us thrown,
> Dotting the shoreless watery wild,
> We mortal millions live *alone*.
> The islands feel the enclasping flow,
> And then their endless bounds they know.

And as the poet contemplates the fact of separation
between man and man on islands of isolation, he asks:

> Who ordered that their longing's fire
> Should be, as soon as kindled, cooled?
>
> *   *   *
>
> And bade between their shores to be
> The unplumbed, salt, estranging sea.[11]

Yet the poet's question is already a pointer to the
basic flaw in the atheist philosopher's analysis of the
human problem. For the Stoic—and our contemporary
secular existentialism can be called a revived Stoicism
—withdrawal into his fortress of godlike isolation may
be his heaven, and hell the presence of a rival god on
his lonely Olympus. But with this value judgment the
overwhelming testimony of human experience will not
agree. The word "love," despite its tawdry overtones, has

[11] Matthew Arnold, *To Marguerite*.

not entered into the vocabulary of mankind for nothing. Hell, for all except the philosopher-aristocrat, is the opposite of the presence of others. It is loneliness. The ineradicable cry of the human heart is one for release from the prison of isolation, for brotherhood, for communal sharing of life's burdens. We see this longing in the romantic love songs of the ages, in a child's arms stretched out for a mother's embrace, in the comradeship of soldiers on the battlefield. We see it in pitiful guise in the alcoholic's haunting of the cocktail bar. We see it in demonic form in the lure of Marxism, inviting the poor to create community founded on hatred, a hatred which, once aroused, turns back upon itself in the suicidal party purge.

But while the realistic existentialist, from the Christian point of view, is wrong in accepting the heroism of loneliness as the solution to the human problem, he is right in robbing us of the sentimental illusion that love and brotherhood and an "I," truly united to a "Thou," is a possibility for unredeemed man. He may prove to us that without the intervention of divine grace separation and loneliness, but not community, are, in truth, the lot of mankind.

Extra Ecclesiam Nulla Salus

Salvation for the Christian means precisely rescue from his state of loneliness. It means communion. It means reconciliation between a holy God and sinful

man. It means, at the same time, love of human brother.
The title page of the Bible itself announces the good
news of a divine solution to the human dilemma. The
Bible is the love story of God establishing a covenant
between Himself and His lost human children. Its
gospel is one of loneliness conquered, of separation
transformed into reconciliation, and of the miraculous
emergence in history of a community of those united
by an act of divine grace to God and to one another.
If the existentialist analysis is true, if salvation from
the hell of loneliness and the act of bridging the chasm
of isolation between person and person, and between
mankind and the inescapable "Thou" of eternity, is
impossible for natural man, is salvation to be found
anywhere except in the covenant people of God, the
Church? Define the *ecclesia* of biblical revelation as
the community of those who have been rescued from
the hell of loneliness, and we confront, with all veils
torn aside, the awesome dogma: *Extra ecclesiam nulla
salus*.

The entrance requirement for membership in this
saving community of Christian faith is the sacrament
of Holy Baptism. With existentialist insights into the
human problem still in mind, this sacrament acquires
deeper meaning also. The New Testament itself defines it as a realistic death and resurrection—a dying
and rising with Christ. Death is a concept with which
existentialist philosophy is quite familiar. Suicide, some
one has said, has become for him his only remaining

sacrament. But he does not accept death as a possibility this side of physical life surrender. The Christian, however, does accept death in the midst of life—death of the "I" of pride in an act of repentance and of surrender of his will to his Creator and Redeemer. Every true recital of the Lord's Prayer is a renewal of baptismal dying. We surrender our kingdom of self to a kingdom not of this world, and our wills to the will of a transcendant "Thou." The Christian coming to the throne of holiness in repentance accepts even judgment as already covenant grace. This is a dying of the self and a surrender of the proud fortress of isolation compared with which the most heroic Stoic suicide is child's play. Surrender of egocentricity, even in token form in our person to person encounter on the human plane, is well-nigh miracle. Can we so much as listen to a neighbor as a "Thou" without at least some gift of grace coming to us from sources beyond our bidding? I have heard a Christian defined as a man who can listen. Unredeemed encounter of man with man is one of clashing monologues.

Outside the Church no salvation—*extra ecclesiam nulla salus*. Does the argument thus far pursued lead back to submission to this traditional dogma? The answer is both yes and no. The majestic mediaeval picturization of ultimate destinies was not wrong in its insistence upon an inexorable either/or. Man's freedom is a fateful freedom. He can refuse surrender to a higher will than his own and make of himself his own god. "Heaven, which is fellowship with God," says William Temple, "is joy only for those to whom love is the supreme treasure." [12] A relationship with the "Thou" of eternity, and through Him, with our neighbor can be won only by a dying to self. Of Judas it is written in the Acts of the Apostles that he "turned aside" from his apostleship "to go to his own place" (Acts 1:25, RSV). Every human soul can "go to his own place," and, if he so wishes, his own heaven which, in loneliness, will be, at the same time, his hell.

Universalist Possibilities

Define the word *ecclesia,* under the guidance of analogies of personal relationship, as the community of those who, in our aeon or in aeons beyond our ken, have passed through, or will yet pass through, the strait gate of self-surrender and thus enter into a life with God and neighbor; and there may, indeed, be no salvation outside this fellowship of resurrection. So far the traditional eschatological symbols may speak the truth. This is, however, far from legalizing this covenant of grace and from handing the keys to heaven to the institutional Church. The latter, in God's design of election, is the sacrament of this saving covenant in history, called to proclaim the good news of its presence and its coming, and granting to those who enter it in faith a down-payment of its joy. But such election is

[12] William Temple, *op. cit.,* p. 466.

one of witness and not of exclusion. How can we conceive the God whose love embraces all mankind of limiting the offer of acceptance, or refusal, of His love to that fraction of the human race which has had the good fortune to hear the story of the Cross? Foretaste of a kingdom of bliss and of the life in Christ which the New Testament pictures as unmerited gift to the "fellowship of the mystery" (Eph. 3:9) may be the special prerogative of the community of faith emerging in history at Pentecost. A Socrates or even an Abraham or an Isaiah was not privileged to join this company this side of death. But can the Church after Pentecost presume upon its privileges and claim a monopoly of salvation?

It is noteworthy that even many Roman Catholic apologists, although dogmatically still bound to the mediaeval eschatological scheme, are, in various ways, surrendering the doctrine of the institutional Church as custodian of exclusive rights to grace and are accepting in its place a doctrine of the Church as, indeed, still the one Body of Christ, but elected to witness to an eschatological *ecclesia* whose boundaries are set by God and not by Pope or priest or legalized sacraments. *Extra ecclesiam nulla salus* remains dogma. "The Church is humanity reconciled with God in Christ," [13] and there is no salvation for those outside its embrace. The modification in the legalism of the mediaeval

[13] M. J. Congar, O.P., *Divided Christendom* (London: Geoffrey Bles, 1939), p. 226.

scheme comes in defining the "manner of belonging" to the Church. Some of these surrenders of exclusive claims are by now familiar. Dissident Christians, and even unbaptized but justified souls, are said to belong to the soul of the Church, though not to its body. Even more acceptable to the stricter Romanist theologian is the distinction between those who belong to the Church by will or mind (*voto et mentaliter*), having received the baptism of desire, and those who belong in fact (*re*). The doctrine of invincible ignorance also breaks down walls of exclusion.[14] One of the most definitive versions of modern Roman Catholic liberalized eschatological doctrine is contained in the encyclical, *Quanto conficiamur*, of Pius IX (August 10, 1863):

It is known to us and to you that those who labor under invincible ignorance of our holy religion, and who, zealously observing the natural law and its precepts engraven by God in the hearts of all and who, prepared to obey God, lead an honest and upright life, are able, by the powerful working of God's light and grace, to attain eternal life.[15]

The Protestant theologian, nurtured on the doctrine of justification by grace, would not like every phrase in this papal pronouncement, despite its generosity to himself and his Protestant brethren. But he, and we all, may well rejoice in the fact that one scandal of

[14] The evidence for the theological position held by the Roman Church is conveniently summarized, in the volume by Congar just cited, in a chapter entitled, "The Status of Our Separated Brethren" (pp. 221-248). See also Karl Adam, *The Spirit of Catholicism* (London: Sheed and Ward, 1934), Chapter 10.

[15] Quoted by Congar, *op. cit.*, p. 233.

Christian doctrinal history may, by common consent, have been laid to rest—the picture of a vindictive God, rendering verdicts of eternal punishment upon victims of ignorance or circumstance.

Are there dangers in our liberalized eschatology? Yes, there are. The preaching of what has been called "cheap grace" and the promising of universal salvation can destroy the entire moral anchorage of biblical faith. At all costs the Christian Gospel must confront man with his inescapable responsibility: the decision between two destinies. Man must remain free to go to a hell of his choosing, or he was not created in God's image. The Church, in turn, dare not make a gleam of hope for an ultimate conquest by divine love of the last rebellious soul in eternity an excuse for sloth and loss of missionary zeal. Even if death should not close the door forever to a sinner's repentance, St. Paul's words apply: "Shall we continue in sin that grace may abound? God forbid."

The myriad souls of our own time and of past ages who have never had an opportunity to hear the Gospel can be left to the mercy and care of their Creator. Our responsibility is only that of evangelizing witness. But every one of us who has been brought into the embrace of the community of faith, and has had at least a glimpse of a reconciled relationship with God, has the responsibility of accepting or rejecting that covenant. Through our fateful choices we shall one day know that *extra ecclesiam nulla salus.*

INDEX

✠ ✠ ✠

201-1056-C-5